Praise for *Briefcase Moms*

"With Lisa Martin's guidance and support, I have redirected my career to one that has allowed me to truly balance my family, myself and my professional pursuits. Her Briefcase Moms program has taught me to examine and improve the core elements of who I am as a mom, a wife, a lawyer and a woman."

—JAN STEWART, CORPORATE SECRETARY, GEICO

"*Briefcase Moms* is a guiding light in a forest of darkness. Lisa Martin spells out what, why and how working mothers can be both fulfilled and successful. This book gives you the blueprint for balancing your life, livelihood and living. Anyone can talk about balance. Lisa Martin lives it. She walks the walk. Get this book. Better yet, get two and give one away. It's the best gift you can give to a briefcase mom or—for that matter, a briefcase dad."

—MITCH AXELROD, AUTHOR, *The New Game of Business*

"*Briefcase Moms* is a must-read for any working mother—and any of those who love her. Lisa Martin illuminates the way, focusing on practical tools and techniques and the context in which they work. Lisa shows you how to find the precious balance between career, family and personal satisfaction—gracefully."

—JUDY FELD, MCC, CMC, MS, EXECUTIVE COACH, 2003 PRESIDENT OF THE INTERNATIONAL COACH FEDERATION AND AUTHOR, *SmartMatch Alliances*

"I think that one of the most wonderful benefits of Lisa's Briefcase Moms program has been that even when my schedule seemed full and hectic I was committed to making time for it. In a way that was the first step in helping me take some time for myself, learn to breathe and develop a fresh perspective on life. Ranging from bigger-picture themes to smaller everyday issues, I have an improved set of life skills that I am confident will set me up for success and balance!"

—THEA KELPIN, CORPORATE FINANCE AND
HUMAN RESOURCES MANAGER, BAKEMARK

"This book is awesome! Whether you are at the beginning, middle or end of working motherhood, *Briefcase Moms* will inspire and guide you all the way to reaching balance in all areas of life. Using practical, powerful exercises, Lisa shows you how to find the precious balance between career, family and personal satisfaction...on your terms."

—KEN D. FOSTER, CEO SHARED VISION NETWORK, AND AUTHOR,
Ask and You Will Succeed

"As a working mom I have strived for balance in life, often to no avail. Lisa Martin's *Briefcase Moms* gives simple focused steps to getting back on track. In a world where so many people say 'you can't have it all' Lisa offers proof that you can!"

—TAMARA STANNERS...MOM...BUSINESS OWNER...BROADCASTER

Briefcase Moms

10 Proven Practices to Balance Working Mothers' Lives

A Complete Program
of Self-Discovery
and Intentional Change

Lisa Martin

Cornerview Press

Vancouver

Cornerview Press
P.O. Box 30075
North Vancouver, B.C.
Canada V7H 2Y8
www.briefcasemoms.com

Briefcase Moms® is a registered trademark of Cornerview Communications Ltd.

Edited by Judith Walker
Copyedited by Naomi Pauls, Paper Trail Publishing
Cover and text design by Gabi Proctor/DesignGeist
Cover image by GettyImages/John Slater
Author photo by Dina Goldstein

National Library of Canada Cataloguing in Publication

Martin, Lisa
    Briefcase moms : 10 proven practices to balance working mothers' lives / Lisa Martin.

Includes bibliographical references.
ISBN 0-9734560-0-0

    1. Working mothers—Life skills guides. 2. Work and family. I. Title.

HQ759.48.M39 2004   646.7′0085′2   C2004-901683-0

Library of Congress information is available on request.
Printed in Canada by Kromar Printing Ltd.

The examples I've used in this book reflect the stories I've been privileged to share in my work as a life coach for women struggling with issues of work-life balance. To respect my clients' privacy, I have changed their names and other identifying details and paraphrased client file notes and e-mails.

*To Robert,
whose love is the rock
from which I fly,
and to Adam,
who gave me my wings.*

CONTENTS

An Invitation and Introduction

Success Is in Your Balance **ix**

How to Choose Your Cake and Eat It, Too **1**

Practices and Intentions

1. *Simplification* **8**
   Intention 1—Take Care of Mom **9**
   Intention 2—Share the Daily Dance **16**
   Intention 3—Eliminate the Stressors **20**

2. *Lightness* **26**
   Intention 4—Unplug Your Shoulds **27**
   Intention 5—Release Guilt **31**
   Intention 6—Relinquish Total Control **36**

3. *Well-Being* **41**
   Intention 7—Find Joy in Every Day **42**
   Intention 8—Commit to Wellness **46**
   Intention 9—Love Yourself **53**

4. *Discovery* **59**
   Intention 10—Become a Keen Listener **60**
   Intention 11—Claim Who You Are **66**
   Intention 12—Know Why You Work **72**

5. *Alignment* **80**
   Intention 13—Live by Your Values **81**
   Intention 14—Create Domestic Harmony **87**
   Intention 15—Choose How You Spend Time **93**

6. *Liberation* **101**
    Intention 16—Blast Away Defeating Beliefs **102**
    Intention 17—Weave a Child Care Net **106**
    Intention 18—Remember to Play **112**

7. *Protection* **119**
    Intention 19—Believe You Are Worth It **120**
    Intention 20—Respect Your Boundaries **124**
    Intention 21—Rediscover No **130**

8. *Connection* **137**
    Intention 22—Transform Complaints into a Vision **138**
    Intention 23—Create a Sisterhood of Support **144**
    Intention 24—Build Powerful Relationships **150**

9. *Courage* **156**
    Intention 25—Face Your Fears **157**
    Intention 26—Keep the Fires Burning **163**
    Intention 27—Be Fully Engaged **168**

10. *Reflection* **173**
    Intention 28—Craft a Life Theme **174**
    Intention 29—Let the Light Shine **179**
    Intention 30—Redefine Having It All **185**

A Vision and Epilogue
    Healthy, Happy, Balanced Children **192**
    The Briefcase Moms® Revolution **193**

    Acknowledgments **195**
    Recommended Resources **197**

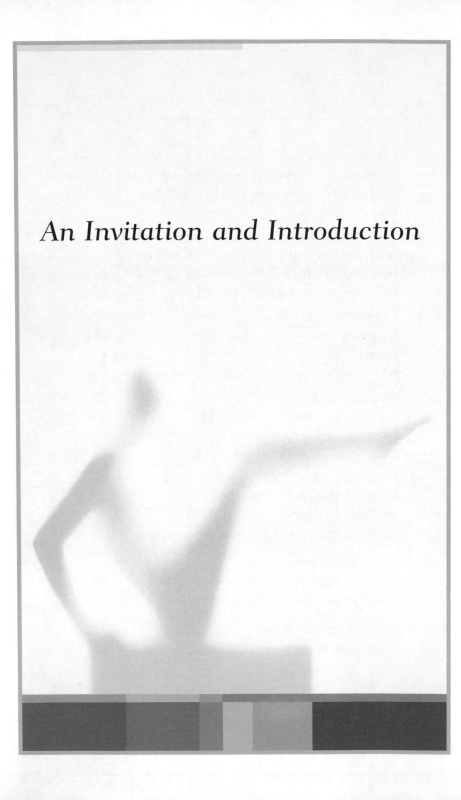

An Invitation and Introduction

Success Is in Your Balance

If your life is anything like mine, your days are juggling acts even the most nimble Cirque du Soleil performer would find difficult. Children, work, partner, child care, house care, haircuts, lessons, family events, meals, car maintenance, friends, exercise, volunteering, bill paying and, oh yes, sleep. All compete for time and attention.

In my earliest days of working motherhood—what I call the Briefcase Moms years—this push-me, pull-me reality of life led to guilt, stress and exhaustion. Many times I wondered, "How can I succeed in all areas of my life—family, career and personal fulfillment?"

The answer, I learned, is in rethinking balance. It is in rediscovering balanced living on a working mother's terms. The truth is, success is in your balance.

I wrote this book to help you discover what balance means to you as a working mother facing competing priorities. Balance, as you know, makes for a masterful acrobat. May you find what you seek in the pages that follow.

How to Choose Your Cake and Eat It, Too

Do you want to find your ideal balance of work, family and personal pursuits? This book presents ten practices to help you balance your life. It provides a complete program of self-discovery and intentional change for working mothers who want to succeed in all areas of their lives.

Just like you, I am all too familiar with the tug-of-war, issues and struggles of work-life balance. These are the ten most powerful practices I have learned through my personal experience of having a child mid-career and in my work as a coach for professional, executive and entrepreneurial women. They will give you the tools to realize your vision of balanced living.

This book is for women whose careers are important to them, whose children—newborns, toddlers or teens—are equally important to them, and whose own personal satisfaction and passion make up the third side of the balance triangle. It's not just about career and children; it's about you, too.

These ten practices have proven to work best in helping my clients find the right balance for them; I know they will also work for you. They are sequenced firstly to support you in uncovering your passions and priorities, secondly to create your balance foundation and thirdly to ensure you achieve success through your balance. Each practice is supported by three intentions addressing your unique needs as a working mother. The intentions provide practical advice and exercises designed for both reflection and taking action. They aim to help you recognize which parts of your life and which choices you have before you will bring joy and fulfillment. Like making the decision to combine work and motherhood, these intentions are both easy and complex.

Combining work and motherhood

Euphoric overwhelm. This is how I felt when my son Adam was born. Powerful emotions surged through me in our early days together: joy, wonder, unconditional love, caring, exhaustion, elation, contentment, pride and relief. This new person shifted all the priorities I had before he was born. But as time passed, I realized that my priorities had only shifted, not changed. I still wanted my career as well as the full experience of being a mother. Some would say I wanted to have my cake and eat it, too.

This cake-having, cake-eating business became a powerful metaphor for me as I tried to figure out how I was going to combine all the external demands and everything I wanted in my life without going crazy. Through my own happiness and heartaches, plus the stories I have been privileged to share during the past five years in my work as a life coach for working mothers, I have come to recognize that you *can* have your cake and eat it, too. The secret is in knowing what kind of cake you want, in choosing a cake you love.

A simple story to illustrate: My son's second birthday was approaching. My husband, Rob, and I had invited a couple of children from the playgroup and their parents, some of our neighbors, the aunts and uncles and grandparents. We had decorated: blown up balloons and even put a small vase of flowers in the bathroom. Food was artfully arranged on platters, covered with cling wrap and placed in the fridge. But the day before the party, I still faced baking the birthday cake. I had probably left this to the last because at that point in my life baking was among my least-favorite things to do (and, to be quite honest, it still is). My sighs of despair and exhaustion (and constant not-so-quiet muttering) probably brought Rob into the kitchen. His was the voice of reason and relief.

"You don't have to do it all," he said quietly. "What's important is that you do what makes you happy. Adam's birthday was meant to be fun for everyone. My sister Lori loves baking. Why don't we ask her if she wants to make the cake?" This was an "aha!" moment for me. I realized that I could have my cake, literally and figuratively, and eat it, too. (It was delicious. Thank you, Auntie Lori.) Who baked it was up to me to choose, but I did have to choose. I did have to decide what I wanted, not just for my son's birthday cake, but also for my life—my goals and passions. I needed to apply that knowledge not just to the little stuff but to the "big" decisions of life, too. I understood that having and eating your cake came down to making choices that aligned what you really wanted with the way you lived your life. It became crystal clear to me that choosing well was the foundation of balance.

Balance on a working mother's terms

What balance means to each woman is as unique as she is. Think about your body, for instance, how you are put together.

The length of your arms, your height and your stride all contribute to your physical sense of balance. This is different from that of all other women and belongs only to you. Having coached hundreds of women to discover their vision of balanced living, I can tell you that embarking on this personal exploration process, on a working mother's terms, takes an approach unlike that for any other because you face special challenges whether at the beginning, middle or end of working motherhood.

Career-oriented mothers come in all shapes and sizes. That's what makes us so interesting. We are professionals, entrepreneurs, executives, free agents, academics and the list goes on. We work full-time, part-time, flextime, on contract, at home, in the office, on the boat, in the plane and at the park. We are in varying stages of our careers—preparing to start a family, managing pregnancy or adoption and maternity leave, planning for our return and returning to work, living the early years (infancy, toddlerhood, preschool) or navigating the school years (elementary to graduation).

As different as we all are, I believe we are connected on the deepest of levels by our shared love for our children. We are connected by the knowledge and experience of the pure joy of motherhood, of those moments of beauty with our children that completely overwhelm our senses in ways we can never anticipate or forget. We know that this time in our lives—when our children live with us—is limited and precious. And yet sometimes, we let the urgency of life redirect us and we are left feeling stressed, pressured...and guilty for not dwelling in the moment with our children more.

Working moms are often experiencing this kind of conflict when they first contact me. They are struggling. They need more time. Most are nearly drowned by waves of to-do lists for career, kids and life—each competing for its share of Mom. They have confided in me: "I want to spend time with

> *Making* the decision to have a child—*it's momentous. It is to decide forever to have your heart go walking around outside your body.*
>
> —ELIZABETH STONE

my children and be engaged in my career." "I want it all—love, success and balance—on my terms." "I've got the flexibility I want but I want a career I'm more passionate about." "I want to restructure things so I can have more time for myself and my kids, but I don't know how." "I feel like something is missing and I'm not sure why or what it is." These women are looking for a new way of doing things, a simpler way. These women are ready for change. Are you?

As a woman on a mission to make it easier for working mothers to live balanced and successful lives, I have heard these sentiments repeatedly from women attending my workshops, surfing my website, and subscribing to my newsletters and e-mail courses. This thread of frustration and desire for change confirmed for me the need for a book that could help. It would be one that encapsulated the principles of life coaching and took a commonsense, reality-based approach to help working mothers manage both a career and a family while enhancing their quality of life—in short, a guide on how to have your cake and eat it, too.

Intuition can guide how you use this book

As you work through this book, think of it as a tool that you can use for change in your life. Leafing through the practices may give you a couple of ideas, but it is in working through the intentions that transformation will happen. In each intention is a Check Your Balance section. Here I ask you to commit to paper your deepest thoughts to help you take action and integrate the intention into your life. As you do the Check Your Balance exercises, you will begin your journey toward better balance.

Inspiration does not beget action. Action begets *inspiration.*   —CHINESE PROVERB

Treat yourself to some fabulous pens, colored highlighters and a journal or notebook to be your companion as you work your way through this book. Large or small, plain or fancy, kept in your briefcase or by your bedside, your journal will be your confidante, your dream space and your reflection in ink and on paper. By allowing yourself the freedom to express your innermost thoughts without fear of criticism or quarrel, you will discover ideas you didn't know you had, aspects of yourself you didn't know were there.

If you use your journal as your traveling companion and guide, it will give you the directions you are seeking. As you become more confident about putting your ideas on paper, you will probably discover that you are tapping into new thoughts, new directions and new solutions. You can be totally honest in your journal. In fact, if you're not, your journal will even help you figure out what is stopping you from being completely truthful. Keep the pages and preserve the trail of where you've come from as you move toward the life you want to live.

I believe the path taken through this book will be a very personal experience for each woman. Following closely the route laid out, working through the practices of Simplification, Lightness, Well-Being, Discovery, Alignment, Liberation, Protection, Connection, Courage and, finally, Reflection is one option. Skipping over certain practices, choosing instead to focus your energy and time on those areas that have been causing you the most concern is another. Some will read the book all the way through first and then go back and reread and work on the areas of most value.

You may be compelled to dive right into some Check Your Balance exercises, while others you will want to think about for a while before taking pen to paper...or not do at all. The way you answer each of the questions and exercises at the end of each intention is entirely up to you. Quick notes, one-word thought-provokers, full paragraphs—whatever form you're most comfortable with will work. You could commit a set time to work through each intention—a day, a week or a month. It's your call based on what feels right to you. You will know it is time to move on when each intention becomes like second nature. Let your intuition guide you as to the best way to use this book.

> *True life* is lived when tiny changes occur.
>
> —LEO TOLSTOY

What follows is not about how to become perfect (no one can be) or how to better multitask and do it all for everyone (too exhausting). This book is about undertaking a process to identify your priorities, enhance your work-life balance, and reclaim your personal power, energy and time. Imagine waking up every morning inspired, excited and passionate about your life.

Your key to balance resides in you. It may be just under the surface or it may be deep down. But the answers are there. You just have to give yourself permission to find them. So, let's find out. What kind of cake do you have in mind?

Simplification

As you set out to define and live your ideal balance of self, family and career, it is important to create some space so you can think about and prepare for your journey. This necessitates carving out some time in your schedule to take care of you and looking for ways to share domestic responsibilities. You need to eliminate the noisy background that stops you from determining what makes you happy, what makes you fully alive to the possibilities of your life. Simplify your personal, family and work life, if only for a short while, so that you can see above the traffic to the road ahead.

Intention 1—*Take Care of Mom*

Intention 2—*Share the Daily Dance*

Intention 3—*Eliminate the Stressors*

INTENTION 1—

Take Care of Mom

Think about your car for a moment. Now imagine, whether it's true or not, that you keep your car in top condition. It's clean; it's comfortable. You've changed the oil recently and you've checked that the tires are inflated to the right pressure. You know you can rely on it to get you where you want to go. But now imagine that over time, as you get busier and busier, you start to take your car for granted. First, you put off scheduling its annual maintenance service. You notice one bright day that the windshield washer reservoir is empty. The oil light starts to come on from time to time. You stop washing it and the remnants of last week's lunch are still in the back seat. And eventually you even stop filling it up with gas. What happens to your car? Well, obviously, it stops.

Funnily enough, the same thing happens to working mothers when the precious gift of self-care is missing from their lives. Many working mothers tell me that they keep trying to "do it all" without paying any attention to their own needs. With no tune-up, no cleanup and no fill-up, eventually you can end up exhausted, overwhelmed and full of complaints and resentments.

Career-oriented moms are often so busy taking care of others that they tend to put the needs of their family first. That is not always a bad thing. Occasionally, even frequently, it may be necessary. But if you *never, ever,* get to come first on your list, this form of self-sacrifice can be a detriment to your own well-being.

Busy as we are trying to fit everything in, we can easily become preoccupied with taking care of the daily urgencies of living. But consider the important foundation that makes your family life happen—you. I know it can be very difficult to put yourself first when there are so many other priorities competing for your attention. The demands of our lives often leave us believing that we have little time or space or energy left over to create something special for ourselves. Not only do we believe we have no space or time left, we can feel guilty if we think of taking time for ourselves as stealing time away from others.

Yet when our needs and self-care fall to the bottom of our priority list, this can be a one-way ticket to an unhealthy and an unbalanced life. Eventually we run out of gas.

Nothing *has a stronger influence psychologically on their environment and especially on their children than the unlived life of the parent.*

— C.G. JUNG

Understanding the theory, of course, doesn't make it any easier to put what we know into practice. Most working moms tell me that they appreciate and acknowledge the benefits of taking time for self-care. We know that we feel better if we give ourselves the opportunity to take care of ourselves—physically, emotionally and spiritually. We understand that the best gift we can give our family and ourselves is a healthy, happy, balanced mom. We recognize that if we break down, then we definitely can't be there for our family. The secret to transforming all this self-care theory into a concrete practice is to give yourself permission to put the quality of your own life at the top of your list.

Become positively selfish

When most of us think of the word "selfish," it brings up negative connotations. We associate "being selfish" with insensitive and indulgent behavior. In fact, *Merriam-Webster's* dictionary defines selfish as: "caring unduly or supremely for oneself; regarding one's own comfort, advantage, etc., in disregard of, or at the expense of, that of others."

Two phrases are key in that definition—"unduly or supremely" and "in disregard of, or at the expense of, that of others." Next time you think about enriching the quality of your life by going for a walk, getting a facial, reading quietly, meditating or taking an exercise class, consider whether these activities must be done in disregard of others. Is taking time to read something you want to read—not for work and not for the children—caring unduly or supremely for yourself?

I believe that such behavior is not caring unduly for yourself, but rather being positively selfish. This is "selfishness," if we must think of it in those terms, that has a beneficial outcome for all. Looking at selfishness from a different perspective will open new possibilities for balancing your life. After all, creating a better quality of life starts with creating a healthier, rested, stimulated you. By becoming positively selfish, you will ensure you are at your best. Being positively selfish means choosing to spend your time and energy on things that bring you joy and occasionally making decisions that are based on what you need instead of what others want. (For more on joy, see Intention 7.)

Practicing positive selfishness is all about letting go of the harmful emotions you might feel because you took some time for yourself. You must believe that by serving your self-interests you will, ultimately, better serve the interests of your family, your colleagues and your community. Being positively selfish allows you to be physically and emotionally present at all times, without resentment.

When Cora began to work with me as her coach, it was probably the first time in years that she had done something just for herself. Cora, in addition to being a new mother in her late thirties, was a successfully self-employed software programmer. When she wasn't working in her home office, she felt she needed to give her babysitter a break, so her lunch hours were spent looking after the baby. Her husband, also self-employed, worked long hours, which left Cora feeling responsible for the majority of the child care. Her life seemed to consist of working on her own, taking care of her son, dealing with domestic chores and sleeping. Just as her own mother had dedicated herself entirely to her family, so Cora tried to as well, while maintaining her career. But she was exhausted, beginning to feel bitter and finding little pleasure in her life.

Seventy percent of Americans say they feel stressed and nearly 60 percent say they are pressed for time.
—USA *Today*, SEPTEMBER 2003

What Cora needed was a little positive selfishness to get her life back on a more even keel. After several coaching sessions, Cora came to the realization that she had never given herself permission to do something just for herself. She

Check Your Balance

Let's start by taking a look at how you can make yourself a priority in your own life. As you open your journal for the first time, quickly reread the remarks on personal journaling found in the introduction. Your journal is for your eyes only, and for your heart only.

Start using your journal to support you in taking better care of yourself. Take some quiet time to consider these questions truthfully. As you begin to write, let your heart lead your pen, and don't worry too much about getting to the answer right away. It is in considering the questions that your real discoveries will emerge.

- When was the last time I did something just for me?
- In which areas of my life do I feel I need more support?
- Am I making decisions about what I do with my time based on what *I* want? or based on what *others* want me to do?
- Can I imagine becoming positively selfish?

remembered that, as she was growing up, her mother was always busy with caring for her children or baking or cleaning. Her mother had devoted herself to her family and never taken time for herself. Cora discovered that she was unconsciously modeling this behavior. After some initial resistance, Cora agreed to start slowly and commit to spending one hour a week just on herself. Strange as it may seem from the outside, this was a very difficult commitment, taken with many tears as she tried to push the guilt she felt into the background.

To begin with, I requested that she make a list of things she'd like to do, even if she had to ignore the pangs of irresponsibility while doing them. Near the top of the list was a long, hot bath. Her one-hour commitment for the first week was to go "self-care shopping," picking up bath salts, oils and candles to make that hot bath an indulgence rather than a practicality. The next week, she had a delightfully decadent soak. After that, dinner with a friend (which she had not done in over a year) was her assignment, and so on. It was the beginning of a change, and now, many months later, self-care no longer feels like a luxury to Cora. She knows it is necessary to keep her feeling energized, even-tempered and focused.

- What do I think my children/partner/mother/best friend would say if I told them I were being positively selfish?
- How do I give myself permission to put me first?
- If an unplanned opportunity to do something just for myself arose, how easy would it be for me to grab it?
- How would I spend my "spare" time if I only had me to consider?
- How can I carve out some time specifically for me?
- How easy would it be to stick to a regular personal commitment?

- Do I see a difference between "taking better care of myself" and "taking better care for myself"?

Once this journaling exercise is complete, begin taking care of Mom by making a commitment to yourself to capture some time just for you. How much time you feel you can take is up to you. It may be only fifteen minutes the first week. In the beginning, pick one thing you'd like to do, just like Cora did. Add others and extend your self-care time when you are ready.

Eighty-eight *percent of Canadians reported moder-*
ate to high levels of stress due to work-life conflict.
                    —LINDA DUXBURY AND CHRIS HIGGINS,
             Where to Work in Canada? An Examination of Regional
                  Differences in Work-Life Practices, NOVEMBER 2003

Cora is now extremely aware of her self-care and dedicates a
minimum of two hours a week to being positively selfish.

There is no doubt that becoming positively selfish can be
challenging at times, particularly if you have gotten into the
habit of setting aside your own needs for those of others. But
it is possible to put self-care at the top of your list without
being egocentric or insensitive toward others. In fact, when
you become positively selfish, you experience a pleasant after-
shock. You find there is more of you to share with others.

Briefcase Moms Balance Zone
100 ways to take care of Mom

Get your hair done. Talk to a friend. Just sit down in silence.
Feel the wind. Do nothing. Take a bubble bath with the lights
off and the candles lit. Treat yourself to new socks. Take a
yoga class. Listen to great music. Meditate. Do a puzzle.
Make cookies that you loved when you were a child. Leave
work early. Go for a walk. Buy a new lipstick. Hire a one-time
cleaning service for the housework. Say no. Ask for help. Live
in the present...no saying "what if." Have a pillow fight. Stop
worrying so much. Let go of your guilt...you are doing the
best you can. Wear comfortable clothes, especially shoes.

Blow bubbles. Play. Do the Tarzan yell like Carol Burnett. Take a weekend trip. Get a facial. Have lunch on a patio on a sunny day. Buy yourself some flowers. Join a book club. Participate in your community. Stop procrastinating: if there is a project you've been avoiding or one that is in limbo, complete it. Go on a date with your child(ren). Try mountain biking, skiing or hiking. Stop trying to "fix" others. Stop letting others "fix" you. Play a board game with your family. Watch a video. Eat pizza. Go to bed at 9:00 p.m. Sleep in. Sing. Dance. Go to the beach. Listen to the sea. Admire the moon. Volunteer. Turn off the television. Unplug your phone. Say something nice to someone. Smile. Forgive. Let go. Fuel your body, mind and spirit. Be silent. Eat and cook foods that make you feel great. Share meals with friends. Eat by candlelight. Borrow a friend's dress. Keep a journal. Avoid emotional vampires. Cut down on caffeine. Resist the urge to judge others. Have a good cry. Reduce stress by arriving five minutes early for your next appointment. Throw out your to-do list for one day. Play. Take a risk. Paint your toenails. Slow down. Watch a comedy movie. Eat chocolate. Don't try to be perfect...just be you. Get a manicure. Redecorate your bedroom. Go outside. Treat yourself to your favorite junk food. Floss. Know your priorities. When you get stressed, ask yourself if this will matter in a week, a month, a year. Contribute to others. Have fun. Mute your e-mail. Stretch. Drink lots of water. Take vitamins. Nap. Read a book that you've really wanted to read. Romance your partner. Go to the park. Forget the mess and take a break. Feel the sun on your face. Make love. Knit or sew something just for you. Travel...near or far. Kiss. Tell someone you love them. Tell yourself you love you. Laugh.

INTENTION 2 —

Share the Daily Dance

Logistical acrobatics is the best way I can describe the daily process families undertake to get moms, dads and kids where they need to be—work, daycare, school, after-school activities, doctor's appointments, friends' houses—when they need to be there. Life can feel like a constant daily dance of negotiating and renegotiating household and transportation responsibilities. But getting yourself and members of your family where they need to be is not optional; it is essential.

It used to be that the roles of caregiver and breadwinner were separate and distinct. Not any more. In a dual-career family, the roles of caregiver and breadwinner are often shared and interchangeable. Both parents are, as espoused in that infamous '70s TV commercial for Enjoli perfume, "bringing home the bacon and frying it up in a pan." Depending on the circumstances of the moment, the demands of each role may change. My clients tell me they feel like they are constantly conferring and bargaining with their partner. Sometimes working moms feel like they're not simplifying their daily juggling act, but only making matters worse. And sometimes, they feel like this constant juggling is not worth it. But it is, because only through sharing the domestic roles and responsibilities can you each understand the other partner's pleasures and pressures. Through that shared knowledge, generosity and cooperation, you can appreciate each other's contribution and build a stronger partnership.

In 2000, 60 *percent of all married couples had two earners, while only 26 percent depended solely on a spouse's paycheck, down from 51 percent in 1970.*

—USA CENSUS, 2000

Life with children and a career is complicated. Whose turn is it to pay attention to the kids? Whose turn is it to pay attention to work? Whose turn is it to drive? Whose turn is it to go grocery shopping? Whose turn is it to catch up at work by staying late?

Even when you think you've got it all worked out, your schedule or plan might need to change at some point during the day. Your boss might call a last-minute meeting that he wants all members of the department to attend—at four o'clock that afternoon. Do you feel you can call on your partner to pick up the kids in your stead? Your school-age son throws up just after breakfast on Wednesday morning and you recognize he's coming down with stomach flu. Can you stay home so your partner can get to his nine o'clock meeting?

A recent review of Gallup Poll data from the last two years finds that in 63% of households studied, both partners bring home a paycheck, and in about one-fifth of those households, the wife earns more than the husband (18%).

—*Gallup Management Journal*, JUNE 2003

Being able to call on each other for support, knowing that each person's career is equally honored, is key to sharing the daily dance. With this kind of understanding and recognition, your dual careers will rarely become dueling careers.

Keep your communication lines open

Although there will certainly be unexpected additions to the schedule, it helps to have a good idea before Monday of what the week holds for everyone in your family. Try setting aside some time on the weekend to review individual commitments and priorities. Through this forum all family members will be aware that Dad has a major presentation to make Thursday, that you have a school meeting Monday evening and that your daughter has soccer practice Tuesday night. You will not only know that it's "soccer practice Tuesday night" but the time and location as well. That way, if one parent can't make it, the other has enough details to handle the commitment. If you post the week's schedule on the fridge door or in some other central location, then everyone in the family will know each other's whereabouts, and you can better handle changes and additions.

My husband and I have been sitting down almost every Sunday morning for the past four years "to plan our week." First we review what each of us has upcoming on our professional and personal agendas. Then we determine, for each day of the week, who's home for dinner, who's out, who's got what deadlines and who's dropping off and/or picking up Adam from daycare, play dates or his grandparents' house. Once those plans are solidified, we then turn to deciding what we want for dinner in the evenings ahead. Although Adam is only five, he's also involved in the conversation... mostly from the perspective of what he would like to have for

Check Your Balance

Use your journaling time to contemplate how to minimize the challenges of dual careers and ease your daily schedule. Take a few minutes with your journal to ask yourself the following questions:
- Are my partner, children and I communicating effectively about our schedules and commitments? If not, how can we improve?
- Do I feel like my partner and I are sharing our daily dance effectively?
- Do I leave enough space in my schedule to allow for the unexpected?
- Do I begrudge the time I spend transporting my children? If so, why?

When you are ready, take another few minutes with your journal to think about the answers to these questions:

supper. He participates for as long as his attention span will allow him, which is about three and a half minutes. But you can bet he never forgets the days he has requested French fries. What we like about this process, which usually takes no more than fifteen minutes, is that it minimizes unwanted surprises, communication mishaps and misunderstandings, for we all know what to expect from each other.

To further enhance your communication, ensure you can easily reach your partner, whether by cellphone, e-mail, pager or other means. If there are any changes to your plans (and invariably there will be), you need to be able to get in touch with each other in a hurry. Strike an agreement to keep your communication lines open. There's no point in having a cellphone number for each other if you don't keep the phone turned on. Also agree that, if chatting to one another regularly during the day is not convenient, you will only call if it's an emergency and your partner will respond quickly.

- Can I make my routine/ scheduling more enjoyable?
- Have my partner and I established clear guidelines about our individual roles and responsibilities for family obligations?
- How can I reorganize my schedule to allow for more flexibility?
- How can my partner and I better involve our children in our daily dance?

Briefcase Moms Balance Zone

Build in a little bit of time

You will reduce the stress you feel in "keeping it all together" if you can add some flexibility into your schedule. Traffic is often unpredictable, for example, and no amount of fretting and banging the steering wheel will get you and your car through a jam any quicker. Make a supreme effort to allow at least five minutes around each commitment. For example, if you have to pick up your younger daughter from after-school care at 4:45 p.m. and you know it takes 35 minutes to get there, give yourself 40 minutes. You'll be surprised at the calm that will envelop you when you realize that you're going to be comfortably on time. The extra few minutes will also help you to cope with the unexpected—a stall on the highway or a quick stop for gas. Five minutes doesn't seem like much when you're packing up at the office, but it feels like an eternity when you know your child is waiting for you at the other end.

INTENTION 3 —

Eliminate the Stressors

Every Sunday evening around eight o'clock, Mary Ann would experience a heaviness descend upon her. She would feel pressure in the space between her shoulder blades creeping in on Sunday afternoon. As the day drew to a close her jaw would tighten at the prospect of another Monday morning. It wasn't so much her work or going to the office that Mary Ann was dreading. She enjoyed her role as a controller for a professional services consulting firm. It was the piles of paper, the incomplete projects, the stack of reading she'd put to one side, the unopened mail, the unfinished filing and the overdue billings that she found depressing. She wondered if she should find herself another job and added "Look for new position" to her to-do list.

Have you ever found yourself feeling this way about your workload? You enjoy the kind of work you do: it is challenging, stimulating and rewarding. It just feels like there's too much of it. Right-sizing, downsizing and technological advances have all contributed to ever-expanding responsibilities at the office. Having a long to-do list can definitely be stressful, but it's not the number of things on our list so much as it is the unfinished business and lack of organization that are the source of stress. Disorganization, clutter, incomplete tasks and tough conversations that we've put off are "stressors" in our already busy lives.

Forty-eight percent of individuals employed in management-level jobs reported too many hours and demands as a source of workplace stress.

—STATISTICS CANADA, 2003

Stressors, whether physical or emotional, consume a lot of space and energy. For example, if your office is a mess it probably distracts you. The reverse also applies: when your office is organized you probably feel happy and comfortable. As an added bonus, you can find what you need immediately without wasting precious time. When something has been on your list for quite a while, it probably induces lethargy each time you look at it. But when you can cross that thing off, the energy gain is almost palpable. Each time you ponder a project not yet completed or reading yet to be tackled, you're losing steam.

Tremendous amounts of energy are also wasted due to regret, guilt and dissatisfaction. If you've got that nagging feeling that your job doesn't really align with who you are (and you know you don't have time to think about that right now), putting that feeling aside adds to your stress. Avoiding a strained relationship with a colleague and sidestepping conversations that you would rather not have can diminish your effectiveness. And as for clutter, well, it just creates a state of confusion.

Stressors deplete your energy

If you are putting up with numerous things at work, it won't matter how much positive energy you put into the rest of your life. You can concentrate on good nutrition, positive relationships or getting lots of exercise, but stressors leach energy from your personal power grid, leaving you feeling like you're running on empty. Imagine your body as a Styrofoam cup and your life energy as the water filling it up. When your energy level is high, the cup is full of water to the point of overflowing. When you are in this state you feel wonderful, your mind is clear and you have plenty of get-up-and-go to do all that you desire. Then along comes a stressor. Each one is like a

Check Your Balance

During the next few days, take a couple of minutes to honestly assess whether workplace stressors are draining your energy. If the answer is yes, consider bringing your journal into the office to support you in undertaking the four-S strategy—Sort it. Start it. Share it. Stuff it—to eliminate stressors. Here are three steps to get you started.
1. Take one lunch break and, in your journal, list some of the stressors you are currently facing at work. If you are unsure where to start, take an objective look at your surroundings. Piles of paper or objects that elicit a sigh or pang of exasperation are most likely stressors for you. Jot them down. You might be able to reel off your stressors in a matter of minutes, or it might require more time. You may be able to identify three stressors or thirty-three. Quantity doesn't matter; it's the naming of the stressors that does.

sharp pencil tip stabbing a hole in the side of the cup—and out drips the water in a steady stream. The more annoyances you tolerate, the more power flows out of you. And if your energy is constantly seeping out, no matter how much you add, you will never reach a state of energetic abundance.

Mary Ann's cup was never full to the top, and when we began working together, one of the first things we tackled were those Sunday-evening blues. To begin, we took an inventory of all she was up against, including everything on, and not on, her to-do list. Nothing was left out, not even the discussion with her assistant she had been avoiding for six weeks. To come to terms with what was getting her down, she knew she had to stop following her cup of coffee around the office, stop looking at the piles of "must read someday" papers and professional magazines, stop feeling overwhelmed by incomplete client files, stop avoiding unanswered e-mails and stop analyzing where to start. It wasn't the work she was doing that was making her crazy; it was the work she wasn't doing.

Once she had taken inventory, I asked her to divide her list into five columns: client work, administration, human resources (those "tough conversations"), marketing and professional development. She further segmented her inventory

2. Now that you have sorted them, for each of the stressors you have identified (begin with only three if there are many on your list), determine which of the remaining three S's—Start it, Share it, or Stuff it—you are going to apply. Once you've chosen the most appropriate S approach, then list the steps you will need to take to eliminate the stressor. Try to figure these steps out in detail. For example, if you have a pile of filing on your desk, your steps if you've chosen the "Start it" strategy might be to review the files, sort them as active or inactive, determine if they need to be filed in your office or in the central system, determine a deadline for filing, then file them. On the other hand, if you chose the "Share it" strategy, you might collect all the files, recruit the support of colleagues or your assistant, and request they file them appropriately.

continued on next page

and highlighted in different colors the following: 1) tasks she enjoyed; 2) things only she could do; 3) things she didn't like doing and could transfer to someone else; and 4) things she no longer needed or wanted to do. From this list she could clearly see which items she needed to take care of and which she could dispense with altogether or delegate to others. Mary Ann also gave herself permission to let go of the stacks of magazines and professional literature she'd been meaning to get to for months. She set a two-month limit on any reading material; if she hadn't read it by that time, it wasn't important enough to weigh her down.

Mary Ann found it difficult at first to recognize that she didn't have to accomplish everything on her list by herself. By delegating to her team and letting go of total control (more on control issues in Intention 9), Mary Ann was able to free up more time for the work she enjoyed and, equally important, to involve her co-workers in interesting and challenging work. Delegating some tasks also improved Mary Ann's communication with her colleagues. Her assistant told Mary Ann that she used to feel intimidated by her, but no longer felt that way since they started having regular team meetings to discuss projects and assign work. With less on her plate, Mary Ann

3. It's often amazing how a task can be simplified by assigning it a deadline. Parkinson's Law states: "Work expands so as to fill the time available for its completion." If you have only an hour to pack or an hour to prepare a report, chances are you will simplify the process in order to get the job done. You can use this approach to reduce your stressors. Commit in your journal to a completion date for three things you are putting up with, large or small. Sometimes it is easiest to start with a small stressor that is easy to purge and build momentum from there. Be honest about the amount of time you think the task will take and respect that. If the stressor is an ongoing annoyance, such as dealing with a constant flow of reading material or a strained relationship with a co-worker, assess how you're doing with this task in three months' time and adjust your plans accordingly.

was then able to tackle those things only she could do.

Working together, we developed a critical path that broke each task into smaller chunks. She then estimated the time required for completing the task and set some deadlines. She was beginning to see through the confusion and clutter by getting her thoughts about work commitments out of her head and onto paper. Mary Ann was able to get started and to stay on track with her workload. When she could see exactly how much work she had taken on, she was in a better position to delegate and even occasionally to say no to additional work (more on that in Intention 21).

It took Mary Ann several months of conscious effort and diligent simplification to significantly reduce her stressors. From our discussions, Mary Ann realized that she might never be rid of all her stressors and that having zero annoyances in her life was probably an unrealistic expectation. Yet she was still able to identify areas that she could readily work on and is feeling lighter and better organized. So much so that she no longer scans the employment section in the weekend papers.

Briefcase Moms Balance Zone
Simplification has four S's

If you feel that sense of being buried by all you have to do, it's likely stressors are lurking, depleting your energy and your enthusiasm. Think about using this four-S strategy to make your situation more manageable.

1. **Sort it.** Take inventory.
2. **Start it.** Stop procrastinating and do it.
3. **Share it.** Delegate the task to someone else.
4. **Stuff it.** Throw it away.

2. Practice

Lightness

The time has come to unburden yourself for the expedition ahead. Carrying around "ought to's" and full responsibility for your world can drag you down. Release the weight of all the insidious, invisible and irritating things you think you should be doing. Let go of the need for total control in your personal and professional life and feel chaos slide away. When you cast off other people's expectations and stop that inner debate about whether you're doing the right thing, you can create a framework to experience the lighter side of life.

Intention 4—*Unplug Your Shoulds*

Intention 5—*Release Guilt*

Intention 6—*Relinquish Total Control*

INTENTION 4—
Unplug Your Shoulds

For many of us, "should" is one of the most commonly used words in our vocabulary. We say it to our children and to ourselves. "I should call Linda." "You should put your sweater on." "I really should go to the gym." "You should hurry up in the morning." "I should take some more courses." "I should redecorate my living room." "Shoulds" show up all the time—and unfortunately most of us are not even aware that they are there.

It is relatively easy to remove "shoulds" from the vocabulary you use to speak to your children, but it is much harder to take "shoulds" out of the language you use to you speak to yourself. "Shoulds" may have been ruling your life for so long that they are almost invisible. They exist in the background of your mind, directing your choices and decisions. "Shoulds" get in your way. They can make you feel miserable; they can make you feel guilty. They stop you from focusing on your priorities by imposing an outside set of priorities that may or may not be what you want to be doing. In the end, "shoulds" compromise your ability to live joyfully. You can only achieve balance when you stop doing what you think you "should" do. I used to spend a lot of my time abiding by my "shoulds." I was so caught up in the busyness of doing, instead of consciously living, that I'd find myself at social gatherings I didn't want to be at, at the office well after everyone else had gone home or at the gym, and I'd resent being there. I did not want to be in these places or situations, but I was driven by an overriding sense that it would be best if I were there. This was not necessarily the case.

One evening, after a speaking engagement at a deluxe hotel, I had one of those breakthrough moments that really revealed to me how much my life was ruled by "shoulds." As part of the compensation for appearing at the conference, I had been assigned a room that featured a guest spa area complete with gym, sauna, whirlpool, steam bath and hot stone treatments. The hotel facility was gorgeous, and it was complimentary. After my work at the conference was finished, I thought, "I really should go down to the spa..." As soon as the word "should" popped into my head, I had a physical reaction. My hands and stomach clenched, and I knew that I didn't really want to go to the spa. There was power and guilt associated with that "should." After all, the spa was free and the hotel expected me to use it (and I normally love being pampered, pummeled and primped by massage therapists and estheticians). What I really wanted to do, though, was take a long, hot bath in the privacy of my room and relax with hot tea and a book. So that's what I did. It was a simple thing, but a liberating experience because it was me who was making the choice, not my "should." After that experience I made a conscious effort to recognize the "shoulds" in my life.

You must do the thing you think you cannot do.

—ELEANOR ROOSEVELT

Check Your Balance

To attain balance between the shoulds and the wants in your life, begin by assessing how the word "should" is influencing your behavior. For one week, pay attention to when you say "should" and record in your journal the tasks you discover are really "shoulds" in your life.

During this week, when you find yourself doing something because you feel you "should," explore in your journal why you are doing it (what is your motivation?). Write for fifteen minutes (about a page and a half) about your feelings around the activity or task. Use the following questions to get your thoughts rolling:

- Why did I think I should do this? Was it a habit or an obligation to someone else?
- Did it feel safer to do what I felt I should do than to make an alternative choice? Why?
- What would the consequences have been if I had not followed

Turn off the power of shoulds

In all honesty, it took me about a year to reorient my choices from "shoulds" to "wants." Sometimes I still catch myself slipping into old habits and listening to my "shoulds." Yet that likelihood has lessened with each passing month. And I take comfort in knowing that at least now I am not blind to this behavior and I am able to change it.

If I hear myself saying or thinking I "should" do something, I stop and assess my choices. For example, if I feel I should return a friend's phone call in the middle of a busy day, I'll decide based on the urgency of the call whether it is best to return it immediately or wait for a quieter time. I'll also clarify for myself whether I want to or am in the mood to chat. And, finally, I'll determine whether my relationship will be compromised if I delay returning the call until a few hours later. It takes less than a minute to go through this process. The result is peace of mind.

Often we run on autopilot, allowing the shoulds in our lives to rule. I have learned that once you've clearly articulated the reason(s) for your behavior, the "should" loses its control over you. I do my best to fill my life with activities that I

through on the "should"?

- What did I really want to do instead of the "should"? (What else would I have liked to do?)

At the end of the week, look at your "shoulds" list again. Grab a highlighter and mark those causing you the greatest trouble. Imagine what it would be like to let go of or say no to these "shoulds." Spend a few minutes with your journal writing about how it would feel and what you would need to do to make this happen. With the "shoulds"

you didn't highlight, play this little word game. Instead of saying "I should wash my car," try "I want to wash my car." Honestly assess whether some of the shoulds on your list can be transformed into wants.

If you decide to delve deeper into this area and continue to monitor your "shoulds," you may find, as I did, that you are transformed into a "shoulds" crossing guard. Like the folks monitoring the crosswalks at your children's school, you will become a pro at "Stop, look, listen and learn."

want to do, not just those I should do. It's a matter of attitude. The end result may be the same—I still go to the gym—but I do it because I want to, because I've assessed the options and made a choice.

In some cases you may choose to attend to a "should" either for personal reasons or because you are not willing to live with the consequences if you do not. But even that choice, to do something you may not really want to do, becomes a choice you are consciously making. "Shoulds" mainly rule you from the outside, while choices are made internally. If you follow your heart, you will notice that you start saying no more often to your "shoulds" and yes more often to the things you want to do, which in turn allows your wants and passions, the antithesis of your "shoulds," to blossom.

Briefcase Moms Balance Zone
Become a "should-free" zone

As you contemplate whether you should attend an event, volunteer, make a phone call, plan a dinner party or buy a gift, review this four-step formula to ensure you really want to move ahead. Just like crossing the road: Stop, look, listen and learn.

1. **Stop.** Realize you've said "should."
2. **Look.** Assess your choices.
3. **Listen.** Differentiate between wants and shoulds.
4. **Learn.** Understand the consequences of saying no to the should.

INTENTION 5 —

Release Guilt

W orking moms confide in me that they feel guilty about a number of things—missing their baby's first stumbling steps, putting their children in child care, having their teens come home to an empty house. And these scenarios relate only to their children, not to mention the guilt that stacks up for taking time for themselves, work commitments, personal relationships...and so much more. When it comes to balancing kids and career, you name it and, in all probability, some career-oriented mom out there will feel some shame or blame about it. I'm told that feelings of guilt are magnified when you are physically with your child but know you are not being fully present. You may be outwardly listening to your teen ramble on about her high school politics, but that work project due tomorrow is speaking to you as well. Conversely, you feel torn when you can't focus on your upcoming sales presentation because your seven-year-old is in bed with a fever and calling Mommy to come home, even though his nanny is with him.

Guilt can stem from not living your life in accordance with your own personal standards, expectations and values— what you feel is right and important. When there is a gap between our expectations of self (and of our role as mothers) and our reality, guilt is often the result.

Initially, guilt can be a positive force. It is a warning to us that we need to make some changes. However, if we don't heed those warning signs, if we don't alter any of our time commitments or actions or attitudes, guilt can escalate...and fast. Guilt can manifest itself as anxiety, stress, depression and other harmful emotions and conditions.

Guilt: *the gift that keeps on giving.*

—ERMA BOMBECK

This happened to Danielle, a mother of two young children, who had been recently promoted to senior vice president in a telecommunications company. She loved her job and had worked hard for her promotion. But she was concerned about the deep feelings of guilt that accompanied her new career commitment. She hired me as her coach to help her figure out how she could stop being guilt-ridden and start finding some harmony in being both a mother and an executive.

In my sessions with Danielle, it was clear that the pull between what she "should" (remember those?) be as a mother and her need to be fulfilled by work outside the home was a critical tug-of-war. However, it was a struggle I believed she could step away from. I had coached many career-oriented moms through the process: learning to let go and to release guilt. The secret to Danielle reaching this state was for her to discover the source of her anxiety. It was obvious to her when she felt guilty, but she was unclear as to what exactly was causing her to feel this way.

Check Your Balance

Take out your journal and at the top of a new page write "I feel guilty when..." Now spend five minutes listing everything that comes to mind. Don't edit yourself; just keep writing.

On a second page (or third, if your list runs wild), write "I expect..." Take another five minutes to list your expectations of yourself as a career-oriented mother. Consider what you expect yourself to do on the domestic front as well as at work. Now review your guilt list and your expectations list. See if you can find any connections. See if you can find any gaps.

If you feel guilty about not attending all your children's sporting events, see if your expectation of yourself is to be present at all events. If so, perhaps an adjustment in your expectations is in order. Maybe attending 50 percent of the games is acceptable.

Determine the source of guilt

After some intense questioning by me and private soul-searching, Danielle learned that one source of her conflict lay in the fact that her mother had been a working mom, too. Huh, you are probably thinking, so what's her problem? She knows what it is like to have a working mom. Well, that was exactly the problem. Danielle remembered her mother always being tired and running from one thing to another. As much as Danielle loved her mother and was proud of her pioneering accomplishments as an executive of the '70s, she still felt she missed out on really being with her mother when she was young. Danielle was frightened she was going to repeat her mother's actions and did not want to. Yet she knew that, given who she was, she was happier and a better role model to her children when engaged in her career.

Danielle also realized that she was what some demographers refer to as a Type E—wanting to be Everything to Everyone—working mom. Meeting these unattainable expectations was creating considerable stress in her life. She was short on sleep. She was remorseful because she missed hockey practices and music lessons. She would criticize herself if she was late for a parent-teacher meeting.

Do your best to determine the source of your guilty feelings. Do they come from you, your children or outsiders who criticize your choices? Write a short paragraph, if you can, that names the source(s) of your guilt and ways in which you can release it.

For example, you are feeling badly about turning down a friend's dinner invitation and discover that the source of that guilt stems from personal programming that you must say yes to each request otherwise you are a "bad" friend. Knowing the source of your guilt, now you can release it by acknowledging that saying no does not mean you are not a good friend. Honest communication with your friend about not being up to a party is far better than attending out of obligation and feeling resentful during and afterwards.

Guilt is only another way of avoiding informed action, of buying time out of the pressing need to make clear choices... —AUDRE LORDE

Adjust your expectations

Just becoming aware of the physical and emotional toll these unreasonable standards were taking on her allowed Danielle to reassess how valid her expectations really were. She realized that because she consciously did not want to emulate her mother, she would not for two reasons: 1) Danielle was a different person, living in different times; and 2) Danielle's life as a parent was unique to her. She began to get comfortable with valuing her own special way of parenting and stopped judging and measuring herself against others. Knowing she was Type E, she began to slowly alter her expectations. This was the hardest part for her. She became more flexible—with herself and with others. What really made the difference for Danielle was that she stopped striving for perfection.

By understanding the source of her guilt and proactively addressing it, Danielle released a lot of her negative feelings. She now knows how to limit the power guilt has over her ability to enjoy her life and continues to work at it. From my experience, personally and professionally, I believe that as long as we have children who can yank our hearts out and stomp on them gleefully, we will never truly be guilt-free. I think that is okay, as it goes with the territory of motherhood. But choosing to live a balanced life means we must learn to keep guilt, no matter what its source, in perspective.

Briefcase Moms Balance Zone
Apologize to others and forgive yourself

"To err is human." Many women carry a long list of things they haven't forgiven themselves for. These items range from "stealing my brother's baseball cards" to "raising my voice at my children," with many stops along the way. Along with this lack of self-forgiveness comes its partner in crime—guilt.

If you are beating yourself up over things that have happened in the past, free yourself from this bondage. Write a list of everything you have not forgiven yourself for—and I mean everything. Some of these things you may be able to rectify, and some you may not. If you feel rotten about arguing with your child, for example, make a deliberate attempt to give that child a special hug and apologize. Then you can put that matter to rest.

Other things you feel badly about may be a lot more complicated, but if you can bring the issue to some level of completion, you can begin to let it go. Perhaps you can write a letter to someone you feel you've wronged. You may choose to mail it or not. Maybe you'll burn it as a way to bring closure. Perhaps you can write a letter to yourself forgiving yourself for whatever issue has been bothering you. However you can manage it, try to resolve past guilt. These issues may still be sources of sadness, and that's natural. But guilt weighs you down, undermining your ability to move on. Instead, look forward with lightness. Guilt is too heavy to carry with you for the rest of your life.

INTENTION 6—

Relinquish Total Control

Even though you may complain about shouldering most of the responsibility and want others to do more, do you have difficulty sharing tasks with your colleagues? Do you seek ultimate authority over everything that happens in your department or takes place at the office? If you answered yes, you just might be a control addict.

Working moms I speak with are used to taking charge and getting things done. They have limited time for decision-making and negotiation, and it doesn't take long to get to the point where they think, "It's just easier to do everything myself." But is it? At home and at work, we must consider how much control we need to benefit the situation, and how much we need to benefit ourselves.

Often the more control we demand over our careers, co-workers and workloads, the more insane our lives feel. Trying to be in charge of everything can lead to bedlam. To gain balance in your life, you must be prepared to relinquish total control. (There's a big difference, of course, between relinquishing

Check Your Balance

Is your need to be in control controlling you? If you find yourself constantly griping about having too much to do and never enough hours in the day to get it all done, consider that you may be the cause of the problem. Look carefully again at the nature of those complaints. Are you complaining about what you have to do or the fact that you have to do it all or both? Read the following seven questions and choose three to write about in your journal. For each question that you choose, write one page without stopping your pen. Then move on to the rest of the exercise. Just let your thoughts flow as the theme of control guides your mind.

- Do I feel an internal pressure to be in charge of everything?
- Am I uncomfortable laughing at my mistakes?
- Do I believe that only a few of my colleagues match my standards at work?
- Am I embarrassed if I am not

total control and totally relinquishing control.) I am not suggesting you give up all responsibility, just ease up on wanting to master everything.

> *What* matters most must never be at the mercy of
> what matters least.   —Goethe

The need to be in control at work had Carolyn on the edge of burnout. A mother of two teenage children and a partner in a law firm, she was perpetually working. She was regularly in the office from 6:30 a.m. to 6:00 p.m. and invariably took a briefcase of paperwork home with her in the evening. After supper and homework, Carolyn would sit down and tackle a couple more hours of work. On the weekends, in between karate practice and violin lessons, one day was spent at the office "catching up."

The heavy workload she faced was exacerbated by her view that her associates could not do the job as well as she could. Unintentionally, Carolyn had adopted a belief that was defeating any hope she might have for balance in her life. (For more on defeating beliefs, see Intention 16.) She believed

right all the time?
- Do I have difficulty asking for help?
- Do I pride myself on being able to do it "all" myself?
- Do I feel my way is the only correct way to do things?

Here is how you can begin to let go of some of the aspects of your life that do not demand your total control.
- Identify in your journal one area at home that you want, and would accept, help with.
- Identify one task at work that you

would allow someone else to take over.
- Identify for each of these one person who can support you and commit to asking that individual for help. This commitment to yourself may be a very difficult one to honor, but it is the only way to begin to release total control. Try it, tomorrow!

You may be in a situation where you really don't want to be totally in control, but you have no one with

continued on next page

that she was the only person who could do the job right and there was no point in delegating anything because she would just have to redo it herself anyway. No one else's work could measure up to her standards.

However, total control in her case was well on the way to creating total chaos. Her colleagues were feeling undervalued and frustrated. Carolyn was overworked, began missing deadlines and had just lost her first client in fifteen years.

Delegate wisely

Carolyn wanted to achieve a better work-life balance. She began to realize that trying to control all aspects of her work was having the opposite effect. When we started working together, it was clear that she needed to find a way to let go and relax. We used the four-S strategy (outlined in Intention 3) to identify her stressors and create a plan to readjust her workload. She did an inventory of her clients and projects and determined which tasks on that list she absolutely loved to do and which she'd be prepared to delegate. That's when things started to get difficult for Carolyn. Organizing and sorting her to-do list was easy; she was in control of that. But asking her

whom to share responsibility and authority. You may have no problem trusting in others' abilities and would be more than happy to delegate, if only there were someone with whom to share the load. If this is the case, do some creative brainstorming using your journal. Start by pondering these questions.

• How do I know there is no one to support me if I haven't yet asked anyone?

• Do I need to form new relationships to enhance my support network?

• Am I willing to make some changes in the way I do things?

colleagues for support was something she was unaccustomed to doing. And it made her feel about as comfortable as a first-time skydiver jumping out of a plane.

Often women who are control addicts never slow down and think to ask for help. They are predisposed to handling things themselves. For Carolyn, requesting help was a daunting task because she was afraid of appearing vulnerable or needy. It also demanded she show a considerable amount of trust in others.

> *The average* U.S. *worker logged 1,877 hours in 2000, up from 1,720 in 1976—and more in total than in any other rich, industrialized country.*
>
> —ECONOMIC POLICY INSTITUTE, 2000

To help her feel secure in delegating her work Carolyn decided she needed to lighten up, not take everything as seriously as she had in the past. She began to look for the humor in situations and to give herself a break if things did not go according to plan. Once they saw the lighter side of Carolyn, her colleagues began to be more supportive and involved as well.

With more support on the work front and a new-found dedication to relinquishing total control, Carolyn gradually shed those weekend office hours. By sharing control at the office, Carolyn was able to find more balance in her life.

> *To live* a creative life, we must lose our fear of being wrong.
>
> —JOSEPH CHILTON PEARCE

Briefcase Moms Balance Zone

Get comfortable asking for help

Acknowledge that support will ease your load and make things happen faster. Just to become aware that you could use some assistance and to get comfortable asking for it can be the toughest part. Asking for help is not a sign of weakness, but rather a demonstration of inner strength and confidence. But before asking for assistance, get clear on what kind of help you need and why. Rather than just identifying the problems, propose solutions such as delegating work or sharing household chores.

3. Practice

Well-Being

A healthy body, mind and spirit will make for a smooth transition to a more balanced life. Create moments of joy in the swirl of your life and be fully present to them. View your well-being holistically as a *wellness wheel* that allows you to avoid a bumpy ride while you move forward. Learn to feel good in your own skin by loving yourself and acknowledging your accomplishments and contributions. Quiet your inner critic and loosen her grip on your sense of self. Be-come hale and hearty, content in (and with) yourself.

> **Intention 7**—*Find Joy in Every Day*
>
> **Intention 8**—*Commit to Wellness*
>
> **Intention 9**—*Love Yourself*

INTENTION 7—

Find Joy in Every Day

Mothers find it difficult to articulate the flood of emotion they feel upon meeting their child for the first time. Personally, I felt a mixture of relief and awe, concern and unbelievable fatigue, love and exhilaration. But overriding all these emotions was a feeling I can only call pure joy.

Joy. It is more intense than happiness, bigger than contentment. It leaves you staggering with wonder and hope. Although joy can be found in life's major events, such as your first encounter with your child, it is ever present and everywhere. It doesn't have to last for a long time and can be found in a fleeting moment. Joy is revealed in the hundreds of small, ordinary events we all experience every day. Residing in true gratitude and appreciation, joy exists in each of us, so it is always within reach.

Joy is not in things; it is in us.

—RICHARD WAGNER

However, when you are swamped with the day-to-day responsibilities of caring for a family, running a household and managing a career, you may simply get too busy to pay attention to the things that bring you joy. Luckily, there are easy ways to reconnect with joy if it feels absent from your life.

Feeling joyful is not contingent on any one thing. Joy does not wait for you at the end of the rainbow; it *is* the rainbow. We have become an outcome-oriented society, and I continually hear from working mothers that they assess everything, including themselves, by their productivity or accomplishments. Of course, it matters what the end result is—but it is not the only thing that matters. You can unwittingly forfeit joy by focusing on the outcome—a time in the future when the goal is achieved or the deadline reached—rather than staying in the present and reveling in what you are doing and experiencing.

Letting go of the outcome is not always easy to do, particularly if you have a lot of yourself wrapped up in it. However, by shifting your focus to the present you allow yourself to be consciously aware of and involved in the doing and being, in the daily minutiae and moments of life. It is here that bliss is found.

Pay attention to the little pleasures; appreciate the wonder hidden in the passing moments of life. Small, basic, everyday things can bring you joy—the smell of fresh coffee, the sound of your child's laughter, the beauty in a blade of grass. Make an effort to slow down for just a moment and practice really seeing and savoring all the wonder that surrounds you. Joy can be found that easily. Our children (when they are at their best) are great reminders of the joy already present in our lives. Sometimes just watching Adam play or seeing him smile is an instant joy boost. Each day can be considered a great gift to delight and luxuriate in, rather than one day closer to the deadline.

> *Slow down and enjoy life. It's not only the scenery you miss by going too fast—you also miss the sense of where you are going and why.*
>
> —EDDIE CANTOR

Stop postponing joy

Often I hear career-oriented mothers say that they will be happy when...they have the mortgage paid off or their kids are out of diapers/college or they have enough money in their savings account. They also promise that they will stop working so hard and start enjoying life more as soon as...they get the company finances under control or get that promotion or put out that fire. Taking this approach to life is needlessly postponing joy.

The way to determine if you are postponing joy is to listen for phrases that might come out of your mouth such as "when I get this done I will do that" or "once I've got this I will do that" or "first I have to do this, then I will do that." We delay joy when we dwell in the future—and wait for something big to make us feel good. If you find yourself spending most of your time imagining tomorrow and beyond, then most likely you are trading the happiness of today for some unspecified time in the future.

The main problem with postponing joy is you can't always count on "someday" being there. For Gillian, a communications consultant with a home-based business and three children under the age of seven, finally getting the dog she had always wanted put an end to her postponing joy. Here is her story.

> I have wanted a dog since I was five years old. Five! That's thirty-three years. I couldn't have one growing up because my grandmother was terribly allergic. Then I couldn't have one in university because I was renting. Then I was working

Check Your Balance

Experiencing joy on a daily basis is available to all of us. The simplest way to start living a joyfully balanced life is to clearly understand what is joyful to you. Remember, your definition of joy is unique to you.

Take out your journal and write "Joy List" at the top of a new page. The idea is to detail everything you can think of that brings you joy, from the smallest item to the largest experience—one item per line until the page is full. Some of you will fill the page quickly. Others might need some time. Be patient—the ideas and thoughts will come.

Once you have completed writing your page, highlight in yellow those items that are most joyful to you. Next, highlight in blue the things you are currently doing that bring you joy (overlap is okay). And finally, highlight in pink those things or activities you know bring you joy

full-time and traveling too much. Then I was having babies and trying to juggle the work-life commitment. It seemed to me that whenever I thought about having a dog, the answer was always "I can have a dog when...I move out of the house, finish school, get a better yard, get married, wait for my kids to grow up, etc., etc." Now, there is some wisdom in waiting. After all, if we'd had a dog growing up we wouldn't have had the visits from my grandmother. But it's something I've had on my "Life To-Do List" for decades.

When we recently lost our cat of seventeen years, suddenly we had the option of getting a dog. My husband and I discussed the option at length, and then decided it wasn't the right time, because our youngest is only eleven months old. Then I heard that a friend, who is just turning forty, was diagnosed with breast cancer. Who knows if she'll get to see her daughter grow up, much less complete her own "Life To-Do List." That decided me. I did not want to postpone the joy any longer. So, we picked up "Cocoa," a black Labrador puppy. I can't tell you how good I feel at last to have a dog in the house.

So what if our already chaotic household is now even more chaotic? So what if our youngest is too little to walk

but that you have been postponing. If your page is full of green (where your yellow and blue highlighters have combined over a single entry), congratulations! Joy is a big part of your life already. If your page is full of yellow and pink highlights and no blue, it means you are not engaging in what you consider to be joyful activities. Some changes are in order.

Make a commitment to pay attention to and allow yourself to experience those things highlighted in yellow. Pick one, two or three things to start with for the upcoming week. Gradually add more to your life when you are ready. Your joy is guaranteed to increase with each new day.

the dog? It's chaos with a purpose. The joy I receive from staring into the soulful brown eyes of a new puppy and scratching her velvety soft ears is worth it. The children will learn responsibility (my eldest is already working on her pet care badge for Brownies), I will get in better shape by walking the dog, and Cocoa will have a good home with plenty of activity and rambunctious children to play with.

Like Gillian, you too will benefit if you stop postponing joy and start experiencing it on a daily basis.

You *may delay, but time will not.*
                                    —BENJAMIN FRANKLIN

INTENTION 8—

Commit to Wellness

Your nose is running. Your body aches. You know you got that cold from your nine-year-old. The work project you've been struggling with is due Friday, and you keep telling yourself, "I just don't have time to be sick."

No career-oriented mother wants to give up her precious time to illness. But the reality is, if you don't make time for your health, you will have to make time for illness. And illness, we all know, throws a curveball at our balance.

This is not meant as a finger-wagging "I told you so." Sometimes even the very healthiest of us gets a cold or the flu. But you have a much better chance of staving off the germs that your child brings home, the headaches and backaches that you might be prone to, or the fatigue that has plagued you in the past if you pay attention to your overall wellness.

Many of my clients tell me they spend more time taking care of other people and other things than they do taking care of their own wellness. They make sure their children eat nutritious foods, yet they skip meals when they're really busy. They let their exercise routine go because it clashes with another family member's schedule. They sacrifice sleep staying up late to get things done. If you've found yourself in any of these situations, know you are in good company. With the daily demands you face, how do you fit in exercise, relaxation, eight glasses of water and all those fresh carrots and green vegetables?

Well, I'm loath to say it but there is no magic, one-solution-fits-all answer for this quandary. However, if you start to view your wellness as integrating body, mind and spirit, you will find it easier to make your well-being a priority. I encourage you to use what I call the wellness wheel to see your physical, mental and spiritual health from a holistic perspective. Visualize a bicycle wheel. See the spokes radiating out from the center to the rim of the wheel; these are the activities you undertake to enhance your wellness. Exercise is one spoke. How you are treating your body in terms of nutrition and rest is one, too. Giving your spirit some time to be renewed is another spoke in your wellness wheel.

The objective is to keep your wellness wheel as balanced as possible. Resist the temptation to go to the extreme—overeating or dieting; excessive exercise or none at all. Be mindful of the contradiction between a great exercise program and an unhealthy diet, lots of meditation and no cardiovascular activity, a nutritious meal plan and excessive intake of alcohol. Extremes and contradictions lead to loose spokes and a very bumpy ride. You may not always achieve a perfectly balanced wellness wheel, but if you're willing to listen to your body and your intuition, they will guide you as you move toward well-rounded (no pun intended, really) wellness.

To keep your wheel turning, consider the following wellness initiatives.

Become a strategic eater

The fuel you put into your body can make all the difference to your health and to your energy levels. Practicing good nutrition means learning about food. It does not mean dieting. Understanding which foods give you energy and which rob you of your vitality is essential to being at your best. Be aware of what you're eating and how you're feeling so that you know what foods work best for your particular metabolism.

Start thinking about the size and frequency of your meals. Eating small amounts five or six times a day has proven to be healthier than eating three large meals. This way of eating is easier on the digestive system and provides a more constant, even flow of energy to the body, avoiding the hunger peaks and valleys. Try changing your meal pattern while you're at work so you'll be less tempted to grab that chocolate bar or bag of potato chips to get you through the afternoon. You'll arrive home with more energy to face the evening.

Health...is the first and greatest of all blessings.
—Lord Chesterfield

Take on water

Water is the elixir of life. The problem is that most of us don't get enough of it. If you experience fatigue or headaches in the afternoon, this could be a sign of dehydration. If you work in front of a computer, you are even more susceptible to dehydration. When Cynthia, a tax specialist with three school-age children, decided she wanted to start drinking more water regularly, she bought a case of water bottles and kept them in her office. Evi, new stepmother to a four-year-old daughter and small-business owner, kept a box of bottled water in the trunk of her car along with her running shoes. When she went to work out, she found she could easily take a bottle of water as she grabbed her shoes. If you drive to work, keep two bottles of water in your car. Then you've got one for the drive in and one for the drive home.

Move for the joy of it

We all know that exercise is good for our wellness. We know that regular exercise reduces stress, decreases cholesterol levels, lowers blood pressure, builds bone and muscle, strengthens our immune system and improves the health of our heart. Even though we know all this, we still find it challenging, if not downright impossible, to find the time for regular exercise. Many of us have started "exercise programs" with the best of intentions, only to find ourselves three months later recognizing that somehow the exercise program has been squeezed out of our agendas. You only have to look at the crowds in the fitness classes in January and compare them to the turnout in April to know that you are not alone.

If your exercise program feels like a "should," it most likely won't last long. If it starts out way too big—with you telling yourself you are going to go to the gym three times a week, no matter what, when you haven't gone in years—there is a high probability you won't sustain it. Yet I know many working mothers who successfully commit to consistent and regular exercise. Their secret weapon is exercise that is joy-based physical activity and can be easily incorporated into existing daily routines.

After years of trying to find an exercise program that worked, Sandra was finally able to integrate fitness into her life when she rediscovered one of her passions. A corporate executive and mother of two, she'd been diligently trying different classes and gyms, with little or no success. I suggested that what she needed was to find physical movement that brought her joy. Working with her journal, she tried to remember what she loved to do as child, what kind of movement had been fun for her.

As a young girl, she hadn't been concerned about "getting in shape" or keeping off the pounds. She just loved to dance. She was in tap and ballet in elementary school, and jazz dance in high school. In her university days she used to go out dancing with girlfriends. She could dance all night, she recalled.

To bring joyful movement back into her life, Sandra agreed to start with small steps. She committed to dance for a few minutes a day—in her living room. Pretty soon her children, still young enough to have fun dancing in the living room with their mom, were joining in. Before she knew it, she was working up a sweat. She liked it so much she began researching dance classes. Exercise was no longer a "should" for Sandra; it became something she loved and wanted to do.

I found it difficult to establish a fitness routine that worked for me after Adam was born. I tried all different combinations: mountain biking on Sundays with weight training on Wednesdays; yoga on Monday nights with ball Pilates on Thursday mornings; a personal trainer. Although I enjoyed these activities, I didn't stick to any one thing. My challenge was I couldn't seem to find a way to incorporate exercise into

Check Your Balance

To learn more about your wellness wheel, in your journal create a dialogue with your body. Start by asking your body the question, "Okay, team, how are all the different parts of you feeling right now?" Your neck might give you one answer, your hips another. Try to pay attention to each of the parts of your body as they each get their moment to report in.

Next ask the question, "Okay, which one of you needs the most attention this next week?" Your legs might answer that they need a really good run, or your shoulders might request a massage.

Ask "Which one of you feels really attractive right now? Which one of you feels neglected?" Write down the conversations you're having with your body team. You will be surprised how much your

my daily routine...and I desperately wanted to, because I knew that I felt better, had more energy and slept more deeply when engaged in regular physical activity.

> *A nine-month study of eighty executives found that those who worked out regularly improved their fitness by 22 percent and demonstrated a 70 percent improvement in their ability to make complex decisions as compared with non-exercisers.*
>
> —HEALTH AND HIGH PERFORMANCE, 1991

When Adam was four years old, my mother told me about a fitness facility designed specifically for women called Curves. It had developed a thirty-minute circuit workout, combining weight training with cardiovascular stations, which sounded perfect for my lifestyle. Fast-forward to today, and I am pleased to tell you that I have been able to consistently work out three mornings a week for the past eighteen months, because I found a system that was complementary to my regular routine. I get out of bed, throw on my workout gear, check my e-mail, then make the five-minute drive to the gym.

body will talk back to you, given half a chance. You will be more surprised as you go about your daily life during the next week how you begin to pay attention to those parts that spoke up.

Write for twenty minutes in total for this exercise. That's long enough to let your body have its say.

Thirty-five minutes later I'm home again just in time to bid Rob good-bye and wake up Adam. The Curves program made it easy for me to incorporate regular exercise into my day.

Relax, refresh and rejuvenate

Ah, relaxation. If you are craving some downtime but not sure where to find it in the midst of all you do and want to do, try starting with five minutes. When you first wake in the morning, instead of rolling out of bed and jumping right into your day, just lie there. Lie there for a full five minutes. Just breathe and think of your day ahead. Think of one thing you can do that day that will be joyful for you. Breathe. Connect with yourself. Breathe again.

And remember, don't beat yourself up if you don't always manage to get enough sleep, eat properly and exercise. It happens, that's life—a busy working mother's life.

Briefcase Moms Balance Zone
Stop sacrificing sleep

Sleep is a necessity, not a luxury. Our mind, body and spirit require rest to feel restored and energized. Try to follow these tips for a good night's sleep:
• Create a bedtime ritual.
• If possible, go to bed and awake at the same time each day.
• Forgo caffeine after 3:00 p.m.
• Do your vigorous exercise earlier in the day.
• Ensure your bedroom is peaceful and calming.
• Keep the TV out of your bedroom.
• Make sure you have a comfortable bed, pillows and sheets.

INTENTION 9—

Love Yourself

On the route to discovering better balance in your life, one of the key indicators of your success will be your ability to become more self-content. This means accepting and acknowledging who you are *at your core* and becoming satisfied—maybe not perfect, but satisfied—in all areas of your life. Achieving self-contentment involves more than standing in front of the mirror repeating mantras like "I am a good person" or "I am beautiful just the way I am." Don't get me wrong. I believe self-affirmation will support you, but getting comfortable in your own skin goes much deeper than that. It is about learning to better understand, better appreciate and eventually love yourself.

One way to develop a strong sense of self-contentment is to give yourself the gift of self-appreciation. Offer yourself the same respect and kindness you give to others you care deeply for.

Feel good in your own skin

I've noticed that women have a tendency to focus on what is "wrong" about themselves rather than what is "right." We tend to pick out, and pick on, the parts of ourselves we like the least. I can't tell you how many times I've heard working moms speak disparagingly of themselves. Sometimes clients make these comments directly to me; other times I overhear these remarks via some discreet eavesdropping. At the gym a woman complains that she has a "jiggle butt." At a fundraiser for my son's school one woman tells another, "I am such a bad mom. I bought a cake for the cake walk instead of making it myself." (It's that baking dilemma once again; I am not alone.) Although these observations may be made partly in jest, they contain a kernel of truth—recognition, on some level, that the woman has not met some outside standard of beauty or behavior.

Whether said as a joke or not, these words can be damaging because the negativity is not only on the surface. These women are most likely experiencing much more disapproving *inner* dialogue, far more than is tossed off lightly at the gym or the school.

You may immediately relate to these examples and recognize this behavior as your own. Or you might not even know that you have negative conversations with yourself. Take the mirror test to find out. The next time you see your reflection in a mirror—at home or in a change room or in the washroom at work—notice if your first thought is a complimentary one or a critical one.

If it's critical (and for many of us it will be), it's time to stop running yourself down. Being happy in your own skin means getting comfortable with who you are, the way you look and what you want out of life. Instead of focusing on what you don't like about yourself, do your best to honor and appreciate what makes you unique. Your smile. Your sense of humor. Do you have wonderful hair or fabulous cheekbones? Now go further. What qualities define you as a person? What do you absolutely love about yourself? Is it your attitude? Resist the temptation to criticize yourself. This is a learned behavior and it can be unlearned with intentional action.

Tara had never been happy with her body. She had spent most of her life complaining to herself—and others—about her perceived imperfections. Tara thought her nose was too sharp, her thighs too large and her tummy too soft. This downbeat self-talk was such an ingrained habit, she wasn't even aware she was doing it.

The eyes of my eyes are opened.

—E.E. Cummings

But when her nine-year-old perfectly proportioned daughter began saying that she, too, thought she was "too fat," Tara was jolted into wanting a new attitude. To support her desire to change, I encouraged Tara to start by playing the "mirror game." Her assignment: every time she looked in any mirror anywhere, she had to admire at least one physical feature—and not be disparaging of anything else. At first this was tough, because she was more comfortable belittling than praising herself, but day by day Tara began to shift her perceptions and see herself from a more flattering perspective.

I then asked her to choose a talisman of sorts, an object that would be a constant reminder to love herself—her looks, her personality, her spirit, her being. She chose two things: a pair of cutout lips formed in a kiss and a bracelet. She placed the "lips" on her bathroom mirror to remind her to "kiss" herself each day. She began to regularly wear a stunning silver bracelet, a gift from her grandfather whom she loved very much. As she touched it or heard it clink against a tabletop or desk, she would remind herself of her inner and outer beauty. Gradually she began to feel more positively about herself, which in turn enabled her minimize that internal unconstructive self-talk.

> *The* worst loneliness is not to be comfortable with *yourself.*   —MARK TWAIN

Stop apologizing for your achievements

Many of the working mothers I know were brought up not to be boastful. However, there is a distinction between bragging and not recognizing our accomplishments and contributions. We have all achieved things in our lives, both big and small, personally and professionally. Oftentimes, though, our inner critic (that little voice inside our head that points out our faults and undermines our achievements) will stop us from basking in the glow of our success. The critic might tell you, "Hey, that wasn't so great" or "You could have done it better" or "You didn't really deserve that." She might say, "Oh, anyone could have done that" or "What makes you think you're so special?"

And if your inner critic isn't enough to contend with, colleagues, friends and family may unintentionally (or intentionally) further drag you down. They may completely ignore your success or not give it the attention you might wish for. Or they might accept your comments at face value when *you* downplay your achievements.

In the end, it doesn't really matter what others think. (You can't control their reactions anyway.) What does matter is what *you* think of yourself; those thoughts are definitely in your control. You have the power within you to honor and celebrate your achievements. When you give yourself permission to feel positive about your accomplishments and refuse to listen to your inner critic, you will feel pleased within yourself. You will proudly share your wins, rather than apologize for them. You might even amaze yourself when triumphal words such as "I am one bad-ass lawyer," "I am the best mother ever" or "I rock" roll off your tongue with hardly a thought. Watch out universe, here you come.

Check Your Balance

1. Take the time to step back and discover how you feel about yourself. Get out your journal and set aside five minutes to write down in point form all your attributes, skills, talents and accomplishments. And, yes, it's okay to boast. If you feel your critic trying to come forward, shut her down. Tell her that her turn will come. But for now, just at this moment, it's your time to shine. When you are finished, review your list, without letting your critic have any input, and make sure you can live with this list for a week. Now make a copy of the list and put it in a place where you can see it every day—in your bathroom cabinet, in your purse, in your car, in the front of your agenda at work. Keep referring to this list all week.

2. In the previous step you intentionally kept your inner critic at

Do the best you can

You wake up with a busy day ahead of you, after spending the night playing musical beds (a version of musical chairs where people move from bed to bed) with your six- and four-year-olds. You and your spouse have "had words" over the previous night's sleeping arrangements. He has left for work in a huff and you're still smarting. The kids are cranky, disagreeable and uncooperative after a night of disrupted sleep. The eldest argues that she doesn't want to go to school because she's too tired. You finally talk her into getting dressed, while you organize her backpack. Teeth are brushed, coats are on and you find your keys. You are almost out the door when your youngest decides to lie down at the bottom of the stairs and will not, under any circumstances, put on her shoes. You snap at her and say things you know you will regret, even as you're saying them.

You take a couple of deep breaths, apologize to your daughter, forgive yourself and let it go. You know you'll do better next time—there's always room for improvement when you are a parent—and you recognize that, under these circumstances, you did the best you could.

bay. Now it's her turn. In your journal, let your critic take hold of your pen. (She won't have this chance again in this book.) Allow five minutes to let her make comments about your list. Make sure you don't give her any more than five minutes. Once she's had her say, acknowledge that this is what your critic says, but not what is necessarily true.

Take a second five minutes and write a dialogue with your critic.

Begin the conversation with "Why would you say that? Have you heard that comment from anyone else?" Listen for any wisdom, instead of criticism, from your critic. Although your critic can be cruel, sometimes there is a grain of truth in her comments, which is her way of warning you, protecting you from any hurt. Use your journal to discern any supportive words versus destructive words from your critic.

continued on next page

Your best is going to be different from situation to situation. It will change depending on how rested you feel, who is involved and where you might be. No matter what the circumstances, the most you can ask from yourself is to do your best...and then remember to acknowledge that what you've done is just that. It is through this self-acknowledgment that you will be released from angst and regret, and possibly see the humorous side of things. You may even laugh about the situation, eventually.

How would your life be different if you learned how to love and respect your body as though it were your own precious creation, as valuable as a beloved friend or child? How would you treat yourself differently?

—CHRISTIANE NORTHUP, M.D.

3. Here comes the fun part. Take a black marker or thick pen and black out your critic's negative comments line by line. As you leaf through your journal from time to time during the next weeks and months, this blackened page will be a visual reminder that you don't have to listen to the damaging words of your inner critic.

4. In your journal, write about one mistake you might have made in the past week. Were you late for a meeting? Did you make a nasty comment to your partner? Were you impatient with your child? In one page (five minutes), acknowledge that situation and allow yourself to move on without guilt, and maybe with a little humor. Go easy on yourself. We all make mistakes.

4. Practice

Discovery

Along the way to a healthy, happy, balanced you, start thinking in big-picture terms. Who am I? Who do I want to be? What do I really want? Not that you'll have answers to these questions right away, but they will encourage you to listen better, to understand who you are being and who you want to become in the world. They will help you get clear on the role your career and your work arrangement (full-time, contract or part-time) plays in your balance. Finally, they will unearth your true longings, acknowledge your intuition and reveal your inner wisdom. Your focus is on self-discovery. Be kind and curious.

Intention 10—*Become a Keen Listener*

Intention 11—*Claim Who You Are*

Intention 12—*Know Why You Work*

INTENTION 10—

Become a Keen Listener

In our search for balance, we might often feel that we don't have time, or don't want to make time, to listen to others or to ourselves. A colleague sits in your office for twenty minutes to work through a problem she has, when you can see right away how she should solve the issue. You've had the day from hell and your partner doesn't seem to notice you're tired and irritable yourself as he goes on about a difficult meeting he was forced to endure that afternoon. You want to mull over a decision, but you have no time to think about it let alone ask yourself how you feel about it.

Listening well is easier said than done. But if you learn these internal and external listening skills, I guarantee you'll be a better decision-maker and communicate more effectively.

Use intuition as your inner compass

Being a keen listener starts with paying attention to yourself—your own inner words of wisdom. Most of us talk to ourselves (in my case sometimes a little too loudly), but do we practice positive two-way communication with ourselves? Are we listening to our deepest desires and dreams and understanding what is truly in our hearts? Listening to yourself is about connecting with your wise self. Not to be confused with your critic, mentioned in Intention 9, your wise self is that little voice that wants to guide you to your right life.

Working mothers tell me that they recognize the power of their intuition and how valuable it can be in steering their lives in the right direction. Even without any tangible evidence, they will often say "Women's intuition" by way of self-congratulation when things go their way. Intuition may appear to be random thoughts or the beginning of a subtle knowing. It's a melody that's been running through your head for a couple of days or that forewarning you've been pushing to the back of your mind. It often begins not as a loud scream but rather as an inkling that something is not right or, conversely, that something feels good.

These rambling thoughts may not take shape as well-formed arguments for or against something in your life, but you need to pay attention to them nevertheless. When we listen to these messages and follow through with our "gut" feeling, things usually work in our favor. On the other hand, when we don't take time to listen to our wise voice, there's a strong possibility we may make decisions that are not in our best interest.

Sue, a controller for a high-tech company and mother of three boys, eight, eleven and fourteen, had been looking half-heartedly for a new job in accounting for some time. After a few coaching sessions, she recognized what her intuition had been telling her all along. While her head told her that a new job was the answer, her heart and gut told her that it was her accounting career itself that was not fulfilling her needs. Here is what she learned from herself.

> For years my hour and a half daily commute time was spent listening to the car radio. It was my "zone out," my "white noise" time. While I was struggling with what to do next in my career, I decided to try something different. I turned off the radio and began to listen to myself.
>
> I purposefully moved past the same old issues such as how was my son coping with his reading difficulties, what was I going to with that problematic employee—and tapped into what my own wisdom was communicating about my career choices. My head (the logical side of me) was telling me to stay in the financial field, yet every time I started to

think about it, I felt emotionally blank. When I let my mind start to consider other options, I felt relief and a sense of possibility. My inner voice was telling me that I wanted to head in a different direction. I began to pay attention to what felt right and good to me. I learned that what I really wanted was to shift from the financial world to the health and wellness industry.

Hearing the messages our intuition is sending enables us to make clear and effective decisions. We direct our lives positively with the confidence that we are doing the right thing.

Hello darkness, my old friend,
I've come to talk with you again,
Because a vision softly creeping,
left its seeds while I was sleeping,
And the vision that was planted in my brain
still remains
within The Sound Of Silence.

—SIMON AND GARFUNKEL, *"The Sound of Silence"*

Create space for your thoughts

Making space in your life to listen to yourself will enhance your ability to learn from your intuition. Stopping the busyness of your life, even for a few minutes, to be with the silence surrounding you will promote a still and quiet mind. When you are in this state, true reflection can take place.

To hear the inner workings of your soul, you must also practice patience. This may mean letting go of your need for instant answers to mirror the speedy pace of your life. Sometimes it is enough to have simply formed the question. You can then let your wise self go to work on the answer. Allow yourself the time to realize your true longings. You may be pleasantly surprised by what you discover and when.

The subject of accessing intuition is inherently fascinating. There is such power in connecting with our true selves. If we trust what our wise self is trying to tell us or point us toward, we will find it so much easier to determine what needs to stay or go in our lives. This has been proven true to me time and time again through my clients' experiences and my own. Intuition might be something as simple as that "little feeling I get" when I go to park my car that tells me to go in a certain direction and, voilà, there is the perfect spot. Or it could be something much bigger, such as the negative or positive "vibe" I receive when meeting people for the first time, which always bears out in the long run.

> *What* I am actually saying is that we need to be willing to let our intuition guide us, and then be willing to follow that guidance directly and fearlessly.
>
> —Shakti Gawain

Intuition is like any muscle in your body: the more you use it, the stronger it gets. I intentionally tap into my intuition every day. To hear my soul's voice, I ensure I leave time in my day for introspection. I leave space around my appointments in my calendar and don't book more into a day than I think I can gracefully handle. It is in those "empty" spaces—in between client sessions, waiting for the kettle to boil, going to the mailbox—that I ask myself what I am truly thinking about a problem, decision or choice confronting me. By undertaking this daily practice, I find I spend less time "talking" myself into or out of situations, less time rationalizing my options. I simplify things by listening to my wise self, for she always seems to know what is best for me.

Listen to, and listen for, others

The third step in becoming a keen listener is to make time to listen to others. To practice listening well, you need to be able to give your full attention, resist the urge to interrupt and offer advice, and let the other person speak freely for as long as they need to. Yet as a busy working mom, it's unrealistic for you (or others) to expect that you can drop everything each time someone wants to engage you in discussion.

I suspect *that the most basic and powerful way to connect to another person is to listen. Just listen. Perhaps the most important thing we ever give each other is our attention.*

—RACHAEL NAOMI REMEN, *Kitchen Table Wisdom*

How can I take the time to listen to everyone properly, you may be thinking. To start, consider negotiating a better time to have important conversations, when you can focus without interruption. You might say, for example, "I'd really like to hear what you have to say, and I know I'm not giving

Check Your Balance

1. Are you a keen listener? Consider each of these statements and then, in your journal, write a short paragraph about a real-life time when each of these statements was true. Give yourself one minute to write about each of the statements.

- I have taken a few moments of reflection time to listen to my inner wisdom.

- I have paid attention to my intuition.

- I have given someone else my full attention when they were speaking to me.

- I have done my best not to interrupt friends or colleagues when they were speaking.

- I have consciously spent more time in a conversation really listening than planning the next thing I was going to say.

you my full attention right now. Could we postpone this until I'm back from my three o'clock meeting?" (Or till I've picked up Johnny from his baseball game or till tomorrow morning at breakfast.) Then make sure you follow up on that promise by bringing up the subject again at the time you've committed to. By negotiating another time to continue the conversation, you acknowledge that what the other person is trying to say to you is important (a form of validation) and promise you will be fully present later.

Then again, some listening is better done without it appearing that you're fully present, because it's just too sensitive. Some career-oriented moms tell me that the best listening they do is in the car, driving a child to an evening event while the darkness provides an intimacy and openness that would otherwise not be there.

> *We* never listen when we are eager to speak.
>
> —François, duc de la Rochefoucaul

Becoming a keen listener takes time and patience; it takes skill and discipline. It takes knowing how to ask questions

2. During the next week, find five to fifteen minutes each day to dedicate to reflection. Begin to listen to what your intuition is telling you. Use that reflection time to write how you are feeling in your journal—no lists, no answers, just random thoughts. Learn to be comfortable in the silence. You might begin by completing sentences such as "I am happiest when..." or "I am calmed by..."

that will open discussion rather than shut it down. But by listening well, first to yourself and then to others, you will find that you learn more about what is important to yourself and those around you.

Briefcase Moms Balance Zone

Keen listening skills

Use these techniques to fully hear others.
• Check for nonverbal cues.
• Focus on what is being communicated to you, and why.
• Suspend your judgment of what is being said.
• Note your thoughts and mention them later.
• Wait five full seconds before you respond.

INTENTION 11—

Claim Who You Are

Working mothers are so busy "doing" all the things that must be accomplished in a day to keep themselves and their families on track that the concept of "being" is frequently neglected. Often sheer necessity, the need to meet all our obligations, drives us to focus only on "what" has to be done—getting a promotion, picking up the dry cleaning, planning a party, running a marathon. The truth is, even our best plans can collapse when we concentrate on only what has to be completed. We must also consider "who" we really are, and want to become, to make changes and bring more balance into our lives.

The roles you play in society—mother, wife, lover, colleague, daughter, friend—are "what" you are. All the things, tasks and activities associated with achieving your goals, whatever they may be, are "what" you do. Your unique traits, skills and talents make up "who" you are. You might be patient, loving, unflappable, confident, intuitive and open-minded. Or you might be better described as "being" curious, intolerant, generous, pragmatic, insecure and lighthearted. You must understand who you are currently "being" in this world to know how you can "become" the person you want to be.

> *Zen* in its essence is the art of seeing into the nature of one's being, and it points the way from bondage to freedom.
>
> —D.T. Suzuki, Japanese sage

Clarify who you are being

When you have a solid sense of yourself, you can tackle not only the daily issues of life with more ease, but your big dreams, too. By realizing her natural skills and talents, Tracey, a college writing professor and mother of two teenage boys, was able to discover her brilliance—her brightly shining essence of self, her true being.

Tracey came to see me because she was struggling to finish a screenplay she'd started years before. It seemed that no matter what she did—participate in weekend writers' retreats, get up an hour early each day to review her notes, enter writing contests—she just couldn't finish her writing project. The challenge for Tracey was that she focused on her perceived weaknesses, which she easily identified as self-doubt and complacency, but she could not articulate her strengths.

When I initially asked Tracey to tell me what she thought her brilliance was, she had no answer. She could not readily describe her natural talents, her true gifts, her special traits. This is a common first response. Many of us find it difficult to instantly name our brilliance, because we've been programmed to focus on what we are not being versus who we are. As a writer, Tracey had continually opened up her work for review. Her peer group tended to comment on what was wrong in her writing far more than on what was right. This critiquing was meant to help Tracey improve her writing, but what happened was that Tracey lost sight of her natural talents. She began to direct her energy toward "fixing" the weaker parts of her writing instead of celebrating and strengthening her brilliance.

To help Tracey recognize her true talents, we engaged in some deep questioning. (See Check Your Balance at the bottom of this page for examples.) This questioning culminated in me requesting Tracey to describe her brilliance, her current "being," in writing. Here is what she wrote: "I am brilliant at recognizing the true essence of people (and situations) and communicating skillfully both verbally and with the written word." By articulating her brilliance, to know herself better, Tracey was able focus more of her energy on being brilliant and fostering her true gifts every day. In doing so, she was able to move forward and believe she could finish her screenplay by committing to a writing schedule that honored her innate talent. In three months it was complete.

Check Your Balance

Start using your journal to begin to reclaim who you are. Take some quiet time to consider these questions truthfully. As you begin to write, let your heart lead your pen, and don't worry too much about getting to the answer. It is in considering the question that your real discoveries will emerge. Reflect on at least three of these questions in writing.

1. Take a few moments to think about your personality. This gets at the heart of who you are, or at least who you suppose yourself to be. Can you come up with three words that identify you and that you have known to be true for most of your adult life? For example, would you describe yourself as easygoing, empathetic, organ-

> ▌ *The privilege* of a lifetime is being who you are.
> ▌ —JOSEPH CAMPBELL

Understand who you need to become

Sometimes, clarifying your true being isn't enough to catapult you forward in your life. Sometimes, it is only half the equation. You must also understand who you need to become to transform your life.

Georgia, a clothes designer, had been struggling with her weight since the birth of her first child. She desperately wanted to get back in shape and generate the energy to keep up with her kids. She had developed her list of "what" she felt she needed to do to shed a few pounds: go to the gym three times a week; drink four bottles of water a day; consume less fat and eat more fruits; exercise with a friend, and so on. The structure for achieving the goal had been created, but she kept deviating from the plan once her enthusiasm faded.

When we reviewed Georgia's "get in shape" program, it was clear that some adjustments were necessary. One reason Georgia's plan was failing was because it contained little joy for her. More importantly, though, she had not addressed who

ized, adventurous...? These need not be the only three words you would use, but they will get you thinking about who you are.

2. What do you really believe to be true about yourself? Write three phrases that describe how you see yourself, and give a specific example of each characteristic. For example, do you enjoy and appreciate your wider family? Do you respect those you see around you who are involved in their community?

3. What do you do easily and naturally? Examine what comes easily to you, what skills and talents you have that define your individuality.

4. What have other people said are you best qualities? What do others compliment you on frequently, for example, a great sense of humor, a big heart, leadership skills?

continued on next page

she needed to become to be physically fit—and that was really holding her back.

Being in-between isn't fun, but it's necessary. It will not last forever. It may feel like we're standing still, but we're not. We're standing at the in-between place. It's how we get from here to there. It is not the destination. We are moving forward, even when we're in-between.
—MELODY BEATTIE, *The Language of Letting Go*

I asked Georgia to consider what qualities she would need to develop and nurture within herself to become a person who placed a high value on being healthy and active. To help her identify these qualities, I suggested she look at other working mothers she knew who had managed to make fitness a regular part of their lives. What qualities did they possess—determination, focus, passion, patience? I then requested that Georgia craft a "becoming declaration," a definition of who she needed to become, the metamorphosis she needed to undertake, to make lasting change. Creating this declaration enabled Georgia to see past the "whats" in her fitness program and refocus her efforts

5. Where do you get your energy? Examine what makes you feel at your best. It could be exercise, work you are passionate about, playing with your children, singing...

6. How do you want your children to remember you? If you were to overhear a conversation in which they described you to someone else, what would you like to hear?

7. What qualities or traits do you think you are missing or would you like to nurture in yourself in the coming year?

In reviewing your answers to these questions, put pen to paper again and complete the following statements: "I am brilliant at..." "I am becoming..."

in a way that would ensure she reached her goal. Written in the present tense as if it were already true, her statement read:

> I am becoming someone who is passionate about good health and moves my body for the joy of it, a person who has the desire, discipline and ability to lose weight and maintain a healthy weight long-term, someone who recognizes small changes and is patient to see results, someone who honors and cherishes her body.

Anna, a new mother of an adopted infant daughter, also wrote a becoming declaration. It allowed her to see what qualities she wanted to foster in herself while her child was young:

> I am becoming patient, understanding, helpful, energized and organized. I am making time for physical exercise, time for connecting with my friends and time to pursue activities that bring me joy. I have the energy and desire to be an active participant in the life of my child, rather than an observer on the sidelines.

As these examples show, a becoming declaration focuses on the "who" rather than the "what" and requests you to become more. It inspires you to "be," to grow and expand into yourself.

Briefcase Moms Balance Zone
Entertain the three C's

Reorienting your thinking from the "doing" to the "being"—from what you need to get done to who you are and need to become—takes courage, change and commitment.

1. **Courage.** To discover the truth about who you are, you need to ask yourself some tough questions and open yourself up to candid answers. The resulting insights might be startling and even a bit scary.

2. **Change.** Sometimes discovering who you are and want to be can be painful. You might feel regret, notice missed opportunities, recognize aspects of who you are that you're not proud of, or come to realize that some parts of your life just have to change. This doesn't necessarily mean you need to make dramatic changes immediately. It does mean being open to the possibilities of change and seeking solutions.

3. **Commitment.** To keep moving forward, make some promises to yourself, and keep them. Commit to exploring and taking action to become the person you want to be.

INTENTION 12—

Know Why You Work

It's Thursday evening. It's raining. You've had a difficult week with two team members off on vacation. You pick up the kids from after-school care and your little one has dull eyes, a runny nose, a scratchy voice and a cranky disposition. You know the signs—there's a cold coming on. Your older child is upset because she needs new felt pens for tomorrow's project, as hers are all dried up because she left the tops off. (She's told you this about ten times in the space of three minutes.) With two children in the back seat of the car, you head off to the local pharmacy to get some children's Tylenol (because, of course, you've run out), then to the stationery shop for felt pens, then to the grocery store to get some milk (you're out of that, too). Finally, you head home. The kids are tired; you're tired (no, completely drained). You have a report in your briefcase that you've brought home to put the final touches on this evening for tomorrow's management meeting.

And you're asking yourself, "Why do I do all this? Why am I combining kids and work?"

You have questioned why you do what you do before, and you will probably do so again. (Let's face it, we all like to engage in a little self-pity and self-torture now and then.) But the next time you question your choices, you will be glad you spent some time and energy understanding why you work. Looking carefully at the decision you've made to be a working mother will help you be firmly anchored in times of fatigue and strain.

> *Mothers with children older than one look just like other women in the same age group, with 72 percent of mothers and 71 percent of childless women either holding a job or looking for one.*
>
> —USA CENSUS, 2002

Asked why they work, most career-oriented moms I've known give these reasons: financial necessity, independence, enjoyment and professional accomplishment. Most need to be and most want to be working. Questioning the validity of your role as a working mother happens mostly in the following circumstances: when you believe working is not a financial necessity (your family could get by with less), when your career is not as engaging as you'd like (more on this in Intention 27), or when you are feeling particularly worn out by your daily juggling act. If you find yourself mentally debating the pros and cons of working, you need to evaluate the contribution your work makes to your integrity, your balance, your intellectual development, your value to your community and your commitment to provide a role model for your children. Is working an integral part of who you are? What would your balance look like if you were not engaged in meaningful work?

Whatever your motives for choosing to work, you need to know in times of stress that they are valid and that they are sound.

Each one of us has different reasons for wanting to work, and each one of those reasons is right for us. If who you are at your core calls for you to contribute to your community, that's a valid explanation for why you work. If your personal standards call for you to continue to grow intellectually, that too is valid. When you ask yourself the question "What do I value about working?" your answers will put your decision into a holistic context. These answers will connect your desire to work with who you are.

Over the last 30 years, reversing previous historical trends, highly educated, well-employed women have become more likely to marry and have a child than their counterparts with fewer educational credentials, even though they tend to start families later.

—KATHLEEN GERSON, PROFESSOR OF SOCIOLOGY AT NEW YORK UNIVERSITY AND SENIOR FELLOW AT THE COUNCIL ON CONTEMPORARY FAMILIES

Check Your Balance

1. Get out your journal and prepare for a little heart-to-heart conversation with yourself.

   Greater balance will result from discovering why you work. Among the most common reasons are:

   Financial necessity
   Self-esteem
   Friendships and camaraderie
   Emotional independence
   Relief from full-time child care
   More balanced relationship with spouse or partner
   Financial independence
   Personal achievement
   Creative expression
   Financial security
   Intellectual development
   Contribution to community

2. On a new page in your journal, write down which of these reasons apply to you. Now add two other

Samara, an executive recruiter for a national consulting firm and mom of a teenage son, has her bad days, like we all do, but on the whole she's very happy to be working full-time. She says she never presented herself with the choice of not working. "I don't feel guilty. I know I'm a good mother. And the fact that I am fulfilled professionally makes me a better mother. I think you have to go with who you are."

Amy, mother of twin girls and a vice president of operations for a printing company, feels respected, liked and valued at work. "Working is the biggest thing I do for myself. I am learning, growing and contributing to my family. And I get a sense of accomplishment from that."

For Erica, a graphic artist and mother of three boys, working lets her maintain her independence. "I'd been in the workforce for fifteen years before becoming a mother. It is important for me to maintain that sense of financial independence. Even though my partner and I work together as a team, I still like to be able to make my own financial choices and decisions, too."

We can do (and we do) an excellent job of mothering while working, particularly when we evaluate and clarify why we are working. But we need to remember that there are no right or

reasons why you work that are unique to you. Decide if you wish to put these motives in order of priority. Are some reasons more compelling than others or are they equally significant? It is important to know your main motivations for working and be able to easily articulate them to yourself and others. Turn down the corner of this page in your journal so you may easily refer to it when you want to.

3. Review the following statements. Pick four that you disagree with the most. For each statement that you pick, write in your journal about why you have chosen that statement and how you might change your situation to make the statement true. Take no more than thirty minutes for this, and try to keep your pen moving so that you tap into your truest feelings.

continued on next page

wrong reasons behind our decision. The anxiety we may feel as we struggle through that difficult Thursday evening or when we read articles that point fingers at "working mothers" comes from living our lives to others' standards. When you discover what your work means to you, you can stop rationalizing your choices and start letting go of any guilt. You can embrace your role as a working mother because you know your choice is best not only for you, but also for your family.

In 1999, 61 *percent of women with children less than age 3 were employed, more than double the figure in 1976. The vast majority of employed women with children hold full-time jobs. In 1999, seven in 10 employed women with at least one child under age 16 at home were employed full-time.*

—STATISTICS CANADA, *Women in Canada*

If you work because you want to, you are fulfilling your own expectations. If you are clear on what you value about working, then you can fall back on those reasons in times of doubt. Remember, no one else can make you feel guilty.

My work is fulfilling and satisfying to me.

My salary matches my value to my employer.

My salary enables me to maintain the lifestyle I prefer.

I have opportunities to grow and advance personally and professionally at work.

The amount of time I spend working is a healthy balance to my personal and family time.

The work I do reflects the priorities in my life.

I never feel guilty about being a working mother.

My work allows me an avenue to express my creativity.

I feel valued and respected by my colleagues at work.

The work I do right now aligns well with my current stage of life.

The time I spend working right now matches well with my current stage of life.

For many of the working moms I coach, the question "Why do I work?" can be less of a concern than "How can I manage satisfying work and a commitment to my family?" Career-oriented mothers share with me that they don't want to sacrifice their family life for gratifying, rewarding work. No one wants to be faced with an either-or choice. They want both. They want the organizational flexibility and support to contribute to the workforce and they want to raise great kids while they're at it.

> *Sixty-three* percent of U.S. children aged nine to fourteen polled in February 2003 said they wished their parents had jobs with more flexible schedules so they would have more time to spend together. Only 13 percent of the youngsters in the survey, conducted by the Center for a New American Dream, said they wanted Mom or Dad to make more money.

By creating a family-friendly workplace, many forward-thinking companies are designing corporate cultures that will maintain and attract top talent—mothers and fathers. *Working Mother* magazine conducts an annual survey of the "100 Best

I know my partner values my financial contribution to our family.

I am happier when I work than when I am not working.

The work I do closely correlates with the things I am passionate about in life.

If you discover that somehow the work you do does not fit with the lifestyle you desire and the time you want for family, look closely at what might need to change to facilitate a better match. Is it you, your attitudes, your beliefs and your skills? Is it your lifestyle expectations? Your job description? Is it the organization you work for? Be honest with yourself and be open to input from your wise self (see Intention 10).

Companies for Working Mothers" that examines these organizations' corporate culture, employee population and policies on work-life balance and women's advancement. Companies are then rated on things such as the work-life programs they offer, the employee usage of such programs and the representation of women throughout the company, plus flexible scheduling, female advancement and child care options. This is a terrific resource for working mothers who want to know more about family-friendly organizations and what they offer.

Companies will see the value of a Chief Work Officer. The simple act of making someone a cwo with authority to improve the work-life experience will alter the playing field. Creating the position sends a message that the company acknowledges the value of providing a workplace that complements, rather than competes with, home life.
—Mitch Axelrod, *The NEW Game of Business*

If the corporate world is not for you, it's important to research your profession and find those organizations or school districts, hospitals and government agencies, to name a few, that offer work-life programs that echo your needs. Statistics tell us that many women are choosing to build their own businesses to balance work and family. These businesses can take many forms, ranging from a dental or medical practice to an advertising agency to manufacturing facility, employing one to one thousand or more people. If you run your own business, you need to carefully consider how to keep the boundaries between work and home clear and manageable. This is particularly true if your business is based in your home.

For me, the right balance of fulfilling work and family life is my virtual business. After many years in the corporate world, both working for others and running my own companies, I decided that creating a home-based business with international reach was ideal for me while Adam was young. Hence Briefcase Moms®, a coaching and personal development company for working mothers, was born. I've set up my business so it can revolve around my life and time with my family...not the other way around, as I experienced in the past. After careful thought and consideration I created a balance vision (explained in detail in Intention 22) and set boundaries around my work, which are allowing me to live my priorities and passions. Maintaining this balance is a work-in-progress, as I am continually evaluating and fine-tuning it based on my current life circumstances. But for the most part it works very well. I am not saying integrating work and family is easy. It is not, but with thoughtful questioning and a willingness to experiment a little, it can be done.

Briefcase Moms Balance Zone
Customize your work situation

Consider what your work needs are, both in time and in satisfaction. Work to live? Live to work? Flextime? Part-time? Work from home? Telecommute? Full-time salaried work? Varied schedules? Permanent part-time? Small-business owner? Consultant? Occasional? Contract work? Freelance? Shift work? Job share? Compressed workweeks? Home-based business? The variations in work patterns these days are as varied as the reasons to work. What is the right option for you? What kind of flexibility are you looking for? What is the optimal balance of income, lifestyle and family time?

5. Practice

Alignment

Do you have that nagging feeling that you forgot to pack something for the trip? If you feel something is missing from your life, the absence could be alignment between what you value and where your time goes. Misalignment, whether it's related to how you spend your time or who's sharing the tasks that take up your time, often results in stress and resentment. As life changes, whether you're on your own or part of a career couple, assessment, reassessment and realignment are essential to your balance. Determine what really matters to you and choose to allocate your time accordingly.

Intention 13—*Live by Your Values*

Intention 14—*Create Domestic Harmony*

Intention 15—*Choose How You Spend Time*

INTENTION 13—

Live by Your Values

One true sign that you are on the right path is when your life is aligned with your values. When you are engaged in the activities and behaviors to which you are naturally drawn and which are of intrinsic worth to you personally, you feel at your most purposeful and peaceful. This is when you are most fully alive and most fully yourself.

Most of us have an intuitive sense of our values. We know when something feels right and good. Articulating our core values, however, can be tricky. Values are a big part of who we are, but if we have to categorize, verbalize or explain them, this can be difficult. Think about times in the past when you've tried to describe to your children or friends what values you hold. What if you could find the right words to label your core values, simply and succinctly?

Gut instincts reveal core values

This intention is set up a little differently, integrating the Check Your Balance exercises throughout. Of all the exercises you do in this book, I believe getting clear on your values and aligning your life accordingly is one of the most critical. So let's get started with the "working mothers' gut reaction values quiz."

Pull out your journal and write these words, in list form, on a clean page.

> *The* longest journey is the journey inward.
>
> —DAG HAMMARSKJOLD

passion
fulfillment
adventure
beauty
connection
contribution
creativity
discovery
feelings

leadership
mastery
pleasure
sensitivity
spirituality
teaching
winning
freedom

Find a watch or clock with a second hand. Now give yourself thirty seconds to circle the top four words that resonate
with you the most. What results is a list of your four essential values, straight from the heart. It's been my experience that this
is an "aha!" moment for most because you have to rely on your
heart, not your head, as to which words you connect with most
readily. You access your core values at a gut level without over-
analyzing and rationalizing. What is even more compelling is
that most of the time, these first four words remain as core values even after scrutiny and analysis. We instinctively know
what our values are. We just need the words to describe them.

Examine each of your four words. Ask yourself if this is
the right word for you. What do the words you've chosen
mean to you? Perhaps you picked "teaching." Does that mean
teaching or mentoring or guiding to you? You need to be clear
about the unique significance of each word. If there is an
alternative word not presented in the "working mothers' gut
reaction values quiz" that represents a value to you, by all
means add it to your list. Remember, though, to limit your
core values to four words.

Write in your journal for two minutes on the first word you've
chosen (and only two minutes—don't overanalyze at this early
stage). Focus on all the variant definitions that word could have
for you. Then move on to the next word and repeat the process.

To confirm that the final four words you've settled on are

indeed your right values, think about how you feel when you are engaged in activities that reflect these words. You might value above all else creativity and connection. So, you feel at your best when you are relating with like-minded individuals and are involved in artistic endeavors. Perhaps adventure and beauty are values you hold dear. When you are exploring new countries, great forests and art galleries you feel whole and satisfied. Maybe you value leadership and are at your best when you're holding a vision for colleagues.

> *Let* the firstlings of my heart be the firstlings of my hand.
>
> —WILLIAM SHAKESPEARE

Once you have finalized your four values and found some appropriate language to name them, post these four words where you can see them. Put them on a bulletin board in your office, in your appointment book or near your home alarm system panel. This way you can reflect on your values for a few minutes each day. Making decisions and choices that keep you on track, or set you back on track, will be easier and faster when you check those choices against your core values— these four words that hold a powerful internal meaning.

When I discovered my values—freedom, connection, discovery and creativity—it was as if a window had been opened for me that I didn't even know was closed. I find it hard to precisely explain the impact learning my true values had on me, other than to say it caused a huge shift in the way I looked at things and set me on a course to reorient my life around them.

That process started with understanding how my values had influenced past choices (consciously or not), how they were currently being expressed, and what areas of my life were in alignment or not with those values. Wherever there was a lack of alignment, I figured out what changes I felt were necessary to enable me to live in harmony with my values and feel truly balanced.

Let me elaborate. I discovered that my love of self-employment is derived from my "freedom" value. When I discovered that freedom was one of my core values I suddenly understood why I had started my public relations business in my twenties. This self-knowledge also confirmed for me why I felt discontented after merging that company with a national consulting firm. By remaining self-employed, I stay true to my freedom value. Knowledge of this core value also makes it really easy for me to say no to full-time job offers, because I know no matter how seductive the contract, in six months' time I will be restless, for my freedom will be compromised.

I honor my core value of creativity by writing and by developing workshops, and on the domestic side by designing and decorating my home. For me to be feeling really terrific, I need to be learning new things and meeting new people— the discovery value. Relating with others is also a high value for me, so I need to connect daily with clients, family and friends either virtually or in person.

Core values simplify decision-making

Values can become your decision-making filter system, transforming those heavy life choices into a lighter experience. When you use your values as a reference point and measure your options against them, you arrive easily and without angst at the right decision for you. When the universe presents you with different paths and opportunities, see how they measure up to your values. If an opportunity enables you to express your values, it is worth further consideration. If it does not, it gets dropped from your list. This method of decision-making is simple and effective.

If I feel out of balance, I know that one of the first things I need to assess is whether my life is still in sync with my values. When I first started writing this book, the process felt great because I was being creative on a large-scale and consistent basis. Yet after a few months the project started to wear on me. When I put writing through my values screen I realized that although creativity was in alignment, my value of connection was being compromised as I was spending more time in front of my computer than with people. So I made an extra effort to connect with friends on days when I was doing a lot of writing and I found my discomfort disappear.

My values guide my actions and decisions on a daily basis. As a result, my life feels easier and I am happier as a result. I know that when my values provide a foundation for my life choices, I am headed in the right direction and I feel inspired.

Close your values gap

If the values you hold close are not being expressed in your day-to-day living you can feel discontented—perhaps even a little anxious. At first, it may be difficult to put your finger on exactly what is wrong. Maybe you've achieved more success than you expected, yet you feel as if something is still missing. Maybe you find less and less satisfaction in what you do, and why you do it. Maybe you find yourself blaming others or angry with people far more than is warranted. There is a strong possibility that you are experiencing a values gap. To understand the depth and width of this ravine, you need to perform a values gap analysis.

This analysis requires you to take an honest look at how your core values are showing up in your life. Take the four words you have chosen and write each of them at the top of a clean page in your journal. Divide each page into three columns. Label the left-hand column "How my value is being expressed in my life." Label the middle column "How I would

like my value to be expressed in my life." Label the third column "Actions I could take to align my life with my values."
Your actions need to be as specific as possible. Fill in the
chart for the next twenty minutes. Below is an example of
what two pages might look life for two core values.

This is only an introduction to what can be a life-altering
exercise, so let your mind and your pen run free. You can (and
I hope you do) revisit this exercise again and again, but for
now, just see how close you are to where you want to be. You
may well be closer than you think, because intuitively you
already know your values.

Briefcase Moms Balance Zone

Values gap analysis chart

Discovery

How my value is being expressed in my life	How I would like my value to be expressed in my life	Actions I could take to align my life with my values
Learning new software program at work Reading biography of Charles Mingus Reading magazines Keeping up with current events	Learning something new every day Meeting interesting people I can learn from Being curious about everything	Travel three times a year Take a course on a new subject annually Join a book club Take on a new role at work

Creativity

How my value is being expressed in my life	How I would like my value to be expressed in my life	Actions I could take to align my life with my values
Not really being expressed outside work-related problem-solving	Taking photos Drawing/painting Decorating my home	Set aside a weekly art night when I paint, draw, do photography or visit a gallery Pick a room in my home to decorate and develop a plan to start

INTENTION 14—

Create Domestic Harmony

Have you ended up as the domestic CEO *and* staff? If you answered yes (and not all working mothers do), this situation may not be what you intended when you signed up to combine kids and career...and it may not have been the intention of your significant other either. Chances are that when you became a mother, you assumed the greater role in household responsibility so gradually that both of you are not even sure how it happened.

After children arrive, many women take on more and more of the caregiving and household tasks. Women have a tendency to become the keepers of the mental map of their family's life. Mom is usually the one who keeps track of all the shoe and clothes sizes, details of friends' birthday parties, babysitters' numbers, doctors' appointments, school enrollment dates, hot dog days, sports commitments, and so on. Mom is most often the one who does the majority of organizing play dates, volunteering at school, running family errands, coordinating social arrangements, and the list goes on.

On one hand it may feel satisfying to be the custodian of the family database, yet you may have found that it isn't much fun trying to maintain your professional growth and commitments when you are the only one running Home, Inc. Your own needs may have taken a back seat. You may be so overwhelmed by your home and work responsibilities that, potentially, resentment toward your partner is affecting your relationship.

Balancing household and family obligations with your mate is not simply about splitting responsibilities down the middle. It is about coming to a clear understanding with your partner of how you are going to operate as a working parent team. Both parties in the relationship need to talk to each other about what they want from life and work and how they can best share the responsibility of running a home and having a family. Although this sounds simple enough, many working mothers tell me this is often a difficult conversation to start and to keep on track.

Communicate fearlessly

Some career-oriented mothers fear that if they talk to their mate about more equitable sharing of domestic chores, they will be ignored or the answer will be no. It was this fear of rejection that Sonia raised with me during our initial coaching sessions. Sonia had returned to work full-time as a financial planner after spending two years at home with her young sons. She thought she had solved her domestic worries by hiring a nanny. Although her nanny did the grocery shopping, planned all the meals and prepared most meals, Sonia tidied the house at the end of the day and kept track of all the household- and child-related arrangements. She paid all the bills and handled the interactions between the nanny and the children. Her husband, Tom, was quite happy to leave all this to his wife, for she had been taking care of it for the past two years. Sonia, however, was less than happy with how things were going. Frustrated, she pounced on Tom one evening when she was left to unload the dishwasher for the fifth time in a row.

As she reported the exchange to me, she "ranted and raved that she was sick and tired of doing everything around the house and getting no help from him." Feeling under attack and defensive, Tom's solution to *her* problem was that she quit her job and stay at home with the children. Sonia felt that her needs had been rejected completely. She closed up and soldiered on. But bitterness festered, undermining their relationship. And she was afraid to open up the discussion again.

After our coaching sessions had provided Sonia with some different perspectives and more positive approaches to communication, she raised the issue of household responsibilities with Tom again. When they sat down together for another discussion, Sonia opened the conversation by asking how they could share what has to be done so that both their needs were met. This was an approach that involved Tom more in the discussion, placed him less at fault and allowed him to recognize that Sonia's needs went beyond the domestic front, just as his did. He and Sonia were able to discuss how to gradually shift the power in their relationship toward a more equal footing.

> *Women* spent 12.2 hours in home chores per week— a substantially higher number of hours than were spent by the men—10.1 hours per week.
> —LINDA DUXBURY AND CHRIS HIGGINS,
> *Where to Work in Canada? An Examination of Regional Differences in Work-Life Practices,* NOVEMBER 2003

Learn to give up having it all "your way"

Many working mothers avoid asking for what they want because they fear losing control on the domestic front. When Adam was born, like many new mothers I was overwhelmed with love, accompanied by an equally overwhelming sense of responsibility for his well-being. I really believed that no one—not my mother who had raised children herself or Rob, my husband and the baby's "other parent"—could care for this child like I could. Looking back, I now realize that I needed to be reminded of two things: that Adam had two parents, and that what I took on as my "responsibility" was really rooted in my desire for control. Of course, this need to be in charge ultimately led to my undoing.

I recall one morning when I came into the bedroom to find that Rob had placed the baby on the bed rather than on the floor, as I would have done. In spite of the fact that Adam wasn't old enough to know how to roll over, I lashed out at Rob. "Don't leave Adam on the bed! What if he rolls off? What if he falls and smashes his head?" What-ifs came flying out of me, accusing Rob of being incapable. Elsewhere on the domestic front, I insisted on being the one to bathe the baby, because I did it better. I didn't like the way Rob folded the laundry or cooked the rice. So I did it instead. Not surprisingly, Rob took on less and less. Finally, completely drained, I asked him what was going on.

As he began to explain as tactfully as possible how he felt criticized for everything he did, and marginalized in his role as a parent, I realized that I had created a nightmare for myself. My need to be in charge was compromising my relationship with my husband and it was exhausting me. I had to come to terms with the fact that Rob was perfectly capable of both parenting and day-to-day chores. He might not do them exactly as I would, but maybe his methods could be good enough.

From then on, I did my best to let go of control. If I didn't like the way Rob did the laundry, I held my tongue. (I'm still

---

Check Your Balance

This exercise consists of two parts: writing in your journal and communicating.

- List in your journal all of the home and family tasks and decisions you "feel" currently responsible for. Tasks can include items such as cleaning house, shopping, making lunches, doing laundry, and so on. Decisions refer to choices about child care, children's clothes, kids' extracurricular activities, and so on.
- Draft a list of what home and family tasks and decisions you believe your significant other is covering.
- Do a reality check. In your journal, assess the two lists with an objective eye. This can be difficult! Determine whether your current domestic sharing is really as out

holding it, by the way.) If he dressed Adam in mismatched clothes, I didn't fret (although I still wish I could find a button that says "Daddy dressed me today"). I began to recognize that each of us had a relationship with Adam, and that those relationships were different—and that was okay. In fact, it was more than okay. If I wanted Rob to fully participate in raising Adam and running our household, I also had to give up determining exactly how everything would be done.

> *Mothers* spent approximately 11.1 hours per week fulfilling child care responsibilities, while fathers spent approximately 10.5 hours per week.
>
> —LINDA DUXBURY AND CHRIS HIGGINS, *Where to Work in Canada? An Examination of Regional Differences in Work-Life Practices*, NOVEMBER 2003

Creating domestic harmony calls for not only initial assessment but also constant reassessment. Continue to nurture a teamwork approach by communicating regularly with your mate about each other's and your family's evolving needs. This will ensure you remain flexible and adjust your roles accordingly. When you enlist each other's full participation in

of balance as you feel it is. Write for ten minutes about the contrast (or similarity) between your feelings and your reality. Don't hold back; just let those feelings hit the page.

- In one page or less, describe how you would like to readjust your domestic tasks. If your home-front workload is not as out of balance as you had initially thought, you might need to write

more to clarify what is really bothering you.

Now it's time to start talking. Find a good time to sit down with your partner and ask how you can support one another. Explain how you feel, without blame. Use statements begining with "I" versus "you" and be careful not to be accusatory.

For example, you might say, "I feel very stressed at the end of my

continued on next page

family life, as equal parents—however you may define that between yourselves—most likely you will experience positive change. And you will feel resentment slip away.

Briefcase Moms Balance Zone
Share the family database

If you find you are the keeper, intentionally or not, of the details of your family's life, make an effort to decentralize this information. Instead of holding shoe sizes, celebration dates and babysitters' numbers in your head, share this data with your partner and children. This could take the form of a verbal exchange, listings in your family calendar, or perhaps a "family resource" file located in your home office. Each member of the family can be responsible for updating their information. When your children are very small, updating will, of course, fall upon Mom and Dad.

workday because I feel I need to be home by a certain time," rather than "You never come home on time to help out!" Listen to your mate. Really listen, without being attached to what is said and without judging the content of the message. You might hear something new about them and about yourself.

Create one master domestic to-do list together so you are both seeing the same picture, then aim to agree on a division of labor that will make your lives run more smoothly. Remember that equilibrium does not necessarily mean equal. One or the other of you may be doing more domestically, but as long as you both agree, and both of you get your needs met, balance will result.

INTENTION 15—

Choose How You Spend Time

When I ask working mothers what they want more of every day, the number one response I get is "More time! More time for me, more time to sleep, more time to play with my kids, more time to relax with my partner..." Time. It is the one true leveler. No matter where we live, how old we are or what our work might be, we all have exactly 24 hours at our disposal each and every day.

Each year there are 8,760 hours available to you. Once every four years you get a bonus—8,784 hours. Research tells us that on an ordinary weekday, the average working adult spends 10.5 hours working and commuting (not including the work that inevitably gets taken home either in your briefcase or in your head) and four hours cooking, tidying, picking up milk at the store and caring for children or other dependents. Do the math. Allot eight hours for sleep, if you're lucky, and that leaves just 1.5 hours a day to pursue leisure or joy-based activities. Do these cold, hard numbers sound like your life?

Factor in that weekends can easily disappear taking care of the necessities of life, such as doing the laundry, getting the car repaired and going grocery shopping. (How many of us see our friends at the grocery store at eight o'clock on a Friday night? Oh, how times have changed since our college days.) When you look at this reality, you start to appreciate why time feels so elusive, why there are never enough hours in the day.

Think about how lovely it would be to have time to reflect. Time to pursue your own interests. Time to do whatever your heart craves. Time to connect with yourself, family and friends. Time to recharge and get centered. Most days it can feel impossible to discover that kind of self-focused time.

As working mothers, we cannot actually create time for our passions and priorities. No one can create more time. But we can reorient how we spend those hours, and we can shift our perceptions about what "taking time for me" really means.

If women were convinced that a day off or an hour of solitude was a reasonable ambition, they would find a way of attaining it. As it is, they feel so unjustified in their demands that they rarely make the attempt.

—ANNE MORROW LINDBERGH

This is not about "time management," for time itself cannot be managed. Time simply is. It cannot be shaped, altered or corralled. Sixty seconds is a minute; sixty minutes is an hour. Time is a contradiction: it is static in its consistency and never-ending in its supply; yet for the busy working mom it always seems to be retreating. What *can* be managed are the ways we choose to spend our time and the way we think about the time we have. Both are equally important in creating balance in your life.

Take a time picture

The best way to find out where all your time goes is to track it. How much time does it take you to get out of bed in the morning, after the alarm sounds? To get ready for work? To make breakfasts and lunches? To commute? How much time does it take you to get started with your day once you're at the office? The information you gather will enable you to make some changes. Accounting for your time in this manner for a week will provide you with a very detailed picture. This record will reveal patterns you could not see and periods when time dribbles away. It will identify hidden time and time-wasters, while also showing opportunities to recapture your time.

Cassandra, a chartered accountant, is a single mom of two preteen boys. Between her kids' activities, mandatory professional upgrading and caring for her home, she lived in a constant state of being overwhelmed. She felt she could never find a minute to herself. When she tracked her time for a week, it became clear why her life was so out of control.

> I was surprised to see how little time I had for me. When I added up how I was spending my time, it became really clear that the things that were a priority to me—spending time with my boys and time for myself—were the areas where I was expending the least amount of my time—only 10 hours a week. I realized right then that I needed to make some changes to honor my priorities. I knew if I didn't make time for my emotional and physical health, I was headed for burnout and would be unable to care for myself or my boys.
>
> It took a few months and some serious effort on my part, but I was able to let go of some activities. I cut back on the number of classes I was taking and hired a house cleaning service. I then started combining time spent with friends with time spent with my boys. A girlfriend and I started weekly trips to the aquarium with our children. Now, how I allocate the hours in my day more accurately reflects my priorities, and I and my boys are happier for it. My youngest commented recently that I am in a better mood nowadays and he likes it that way.

Seeing a clear picture of how you spend time gives you an opportunity to make changes that are anchored in the reality of your day-to-day life and thus more likely to be effective and long-lasting.

Watch for hidden time

One of the easiest ways to find more time is to look for hidden time—time surrounding a main activity that we often don't take into consideration. Sometimes, it steals time from a day. For example, a half-hour doctor's appointment actually takes one and a half hours when you include 20 minutes to travel to the office, 20 minutes' waiting time, 30 minutes with the doctor, 20 minutes to return from the office and 5 minutes to get settled back in. However, hidden time can also add time. Discovering the hidden time she had on Friday nights helped Maria, an information technology consultant and mother of teenagers, transform her frustration into a gift.

> With two nondriving teenagers, every Friday night seemed to be spent ferrying my son and daughter to their friends' houses or to the movie theatre to meet up with a group. I wanted to know where they were and who they were with, and I wanted to make sure they were safe, so I was glad to be the parent driving them. But it was eating up my end-of-week relaxing time, too. I didn't feel I could make plans to have dinner with a friend or go out because I had to be available to accommodate their schedules. I didn't have a whole evening to myself. But I did have hour-long slices.
>
> I decided I had to find relaxation that didn't involve other people and that could be interrupted when that inevitable phone call came—"Mom, can you come and get me?" My solution was to set aside Friday nights for video night. I worked my way through a lot of Academy Award winners and foreign films at the video store, films I had always wanted to see but had never gotten around to. It got so that I actually looked forward to Friday nights, knowing that I was doing something for me at the same time as being on call for my kids. I didn't mind pausing my movie for half

an hour, two or three times in the evening, because it was a choice I had made.

Make a concerted effort to identify the hidden time in your life. You never know how many minutes you may uncover.

Dump time-wasters

Have you ever considered that you might be wasting your time? There are so many things we do just because we think we "should" (remember those?). We spend more time thinking about what we are going to do than doing it. We make lists. We overanalyze our decisions, big and small ("analysis paralysis," one of my clients calls it). We worry. We flick through the television channels without settling on anything satisfying. We procrastinate or leave things uncompleted because they are not perfect. We try to do too many things at the same time and end up not getting any of them done. When you start tracking your time, pay attention to those things that feel like a waste of your time and look at ways to eliminate them.

Maya, a mother of two school-age daughters and a sales rep for a computer services company, discovered she wasn't using her time as efficiently as she thought she was.

> After tracking my time for a couple of weeks, it became really clear to me that our morning routine was hugely ineffective. What I thought was taking about an hour was actually consuming upwards of two hours each weekday. No wonder I was consistently late for work and stressed each morning. What surprised me was the amount of time I was taking for my personal grooming. I don't mean the time I took to have a shower and put on my makeup...but the decision time, how much time I wasted wondering what

to wear, which shoes matched, what jewelry, what complementary makeup to put on. I know it sounds crazy, but I realized I was spending between fifteen minutes and half an hour a day just trying to make decisions. My girls were the same, spending more time deciding what to wear than actually getting dressed. So to eliminate the time wasters in the morning, I began putting out my clothes and the girls' clothes the evening before. Now it takes us ten minutes to get dressed. Somehow I am able to make that clothing decision much more quickly in the evening.

The extra time you are looking for in your life may be waiting in the corners of your daily routines, hiding in unrecognized moments and unnecessary tasks. It may be found through enhanced and speedier decision-making. It can be discovered by slowing your pace and focusing on what is important instead of what appears urgent. When you combine a clear picture of how you want to spend your time with the realization that time is a gift for you to squander or save, you can start to create space for yourself and your passions.

Check Your Balance

To find time, you'll need to invest some time. Let's discover where your time goes. In your journal, create a time chart. Use a ruler to draw three columns (two narrower left-hand, one wider right-hand) on several pages. For four days, including one day when you're not at work, track your time in fifteen-minute increments. Note everything you do in your day and how much time you spend doing it. Keep your journal with you as you go through these four days. On the right-hand side of the page write each thing you do in a day, as you do it. Include commuting, working at the computer, attending meetings, studying, worrying, sleeping, being entertained, spending time with your children, flicking channels, surfing the Internet, paying bills, watching TV,

Briefcase Moms Balance Zone
Sample time chart

Use this simple chart as a way to take a "time picture" of your day-to-day activities. Be honest and accurate in recording how your time is spent.

Day/Time	Time Spent	Activity
Thurs 11:00 p.m.	8.0 hrs	Sleep
Fri 7:00 a.m.	.25 hr	Get up, choose clothes
7:15	.5 hr	Shower, dry hair, put on makeup, wake up
7:30		children
7:45	.25 hr	Organize breakfast

being alone, grooming yourself, socializing at the office, doing household chores, volunteering, attending to your spiritual practice, daydreaming, reading, talking on the phone, shopping and everything else. (You'll develop a shorthand for noting groups of activities as you continue with this exercise.)

On the left-hand side of the page note the time and amount of time you take to do these tasks, as you do them. Remember to include all the hidden time associated with these activities. Make sure you track time as you spend it. If you try to reconstruct your time expenditures at the end of the day, you won't be accurate. Once you have entered all the time spent on various activities, total your hours for each of the four days. You will have accounted for ninety-six hours.

Now analyze how you spend

Briefcase Moms Balance Zone

Me Time mantra

It can be difficult to reserve time specifically for you to be alone—Me Time. When you feel that you absolutely, positively can't take time for yourself is probably when you most need to. The challenge for most working mothers is putting aside the feelings of guilt about not being a "good mother" when they take time for themselves. However, children benefit not only from the love and time you give to them, but also from the love and time you give to yourself. When you are living joyfully and passionately, you become more content and peaceful and set a healthy example for your children. Make this your Me Time mantra—"Enriching my life enriches my children's lives."

your time. In your journal, create a list of your tracked activities. Put those on which you spend the most time at the top and the activity that takes the least amount of time at the bottom. Scrutinize this list carefully, knowing the work you've put into tracking your time for the past few days. Check to see if the areas where you are spending the most time correspond to your priorities. No need to come up with solutions right now. The solutions will come with the awareness you've just gained about how you spend your time and about the power you have to align your time with your passions. This will be a very useful exercise as you continue to work through this book.

6. Practice

Liberation

The road you take to create the life you want can be full of potholes, roadblocks and stop signs. These obstacles need to be moved through so you have the freedom to travel at optimal speed. One of the greatest barriers may, in fact, be you. Your thoughts and beliefs may be getting in your way. Liberate yourself from defeating beliefs, from child care worries, from self-imposed seriousness. Know your children are safe and thriving whether you are at work or out on the town. Inject more laughter, humor and play into your day. Have more fun and enjoy life.

> **Intention 16**—*Blast Away Defeating Beliefs*
> **Intention 17**—*Weave a Child Care Net*
> **Intention 18**—*Remember to Play*

INTENTION 16—

Blast Away Defeating Beliefs

As you look ahead to balancing your life, is something block-ing your line of sight? For most career-oriented mothers who are managing many priorities, the answer is usually a resounding yes. As much as it may feel like it, not one of these obstacles, large or small, is insurmountable. Some obstacles can be moved to one side. Some of them time will take care of naturally. And some need to be blown to smithereens.

I imagine you can probably think of several obstacles that are stopping you from living a balanced life. Not enough time. Not the right time. Not enough money. Not enough security. Not enough family support. There are as many obstructions in your path as you can imagine. But that's the key—your imagination. What's most often the biggest barrier of all is you, your thoughts, what you believe to be true. What you think can propel you forward or keep you stuck. If you can just get out of your own way, you can make things happen. It's time to get out the dynamite.

A woman cannot directly choose her circumstances, but she can choose her thoughts, and so indirectly, yet surely, shape her circumstances.
—DOROTHY HULST, *As a Woman Thinketh*

Defeating beliefs hold you back

Limiting and negative thoughts, about you, your abilities and the possibilities open to you, are best described as defeating beliefs. They are often very simple, even simplistic, yet they can have a profound, if inscrutable, effect on our lives. When you are in the grasp of your defeating beliefs it can feel as if you are in a holding pattern, forever circling in the sky, not understanding why you are not landing.

To liberate yourself from defeating beliefs you must first identify them. Pay attention to your words. What do you tell others and yourself you cannot do? Listen to the excuses you give yourself for not doing things. Listen to your fears (more on those in Intention 25). Often a defeating belief lurks behind an excuse or a fear—particularly concerning the things you are most passionate about. "I'm too old to start this now." "I won't be able to make any money doing that." "I have to be in much better shape." "I don't have time." "My children use up all my energy." "It will never work." When you explore your excuses and fears, you will discover your defeating beliefs.

> *It is hard to let old beliefs go. They are familiar. We are comfortable with them and have spent years building systems and developing habits that depend on them. Like a man who has worn eyeglasses so long that he forgets he has them on, we forget that the world looks to us the way it does because we have become used to seeing it that way through a particular set of lenses. Today, however, we need new lenses. And we need to throw the old ones away.*
>
> —Kenichi Ohmae

Uncovering a defeating belief enabled Kelly to shift from focusing on obstacles to seeing opportunities. A lawyer for a not-for-profit agency and mother to a 13-year-old daughter and 10-year-old son, Kelly felt stuck at work and at home. After a few discussions with Kelly I could see there was a defeating belief in her way. In one session when Kelly said, "Whenever I get my hopes up, things don't work out," her defeating belief was revealed. This way of thinking was preventing Kelly from believing she could change the circumstances of her life.

To help Kelly recognize this defeating belief and its source, I asked her to imagine a long wooden table, a harvest table, with four sturdy legs. The tabletop was the defeating belief—"Whenever I get my hopes up, things don't work out"; this surface was solid and steady. What held that tabletop up were the legs she had shoved underneath it. Legs of life experience and evidence she'd encountered herself or seen in others, which supported and, most likely, created her belief.

I asked Kelly to name the legs of her defeating belief, what had happened in her life to make her conclude that whenever she got her hopes up, things didn't work out. It was very difficult for her to identify specific examples to support her belief, although she did name a few—lean Christmases as a child, not buying her dream house. When clients explore defeating beliefs, I find they often have a false conviction that there are many and very good reasons for them to think the way they do. However, when they deconstruct the defeating belief, they discover they don't have a leg to stand on (sorry, couldn't resist that).

Discovering that she had little validation for her defeating belief was an emotional experience for Kelly met with relief, awe, tears and wonder. Armed with a better under-

Check Your Balance

Take thirty minutes to explore more fully the idea of defeating beliefs and power beliefs. Filling at least two pages in your journal, write down the first thing that leaps into your mind when you consider each of the following questions.

- Concentrate on one of your dreams—maybe it's running your own business or spending time at the lake or completing a half-marathon. Whatever it is, can you identify in general terms why the dream is still a dream and not a reality? Do you think you have put excuses in your path that are blocking your progress?
- Can you specifically name two of those excuses? What in particular is getting in your way? These excuses are the key to identifying and unlocking your defeating beliefs.
- Can you rephrase those excuses as "defeating beliefs"? Write down two clearly stated defeating beliefs that you hold.

standing of her defeating belief, Kelly began to think she might be able to release the effect it had on her.

> *Obstacles don't have to stop you. If you run into a wall, don't turn around and give up. Figure out how to climb it, go through it, or work around it.*
>
> —MICHAEL JORDAN

Power beliefs clear your path

The key to overcoming a defeating belief is to convert it to a power belief. Thoughts, words, facts and images that support you and propel you toward your dreams are power beliefs. Like a stick of dynamite, a power belief can blow the obstacles out of your path.

To start this conversion process, I asked Kelly to look for evidence that was contrary to her defeating belief. That came easily for her. She began to list off all the things she'd hoped for and received or achieved, such as a healthy family, a lifestyle she loved, friends she treasured, a flexible career. With these strong alternative table legs in place, I asked her to modify her tabletop accordingly and eliminate the negative

On the next page of your journal, draw a tabletop representing a defeating belief and label the legs that hold that tabletop up. Remember, the legs are your life experiences that support this belief.

Now look for new evidence to support a belief that will move you closer to achieving the dream you have identified. The evidence is out there, and you will be surprised how quickly you find it once you start looking. Once empowering evidence is in place, you are ready to dynamite that defeating belief. Create a power belief by eliminating the negative language from your defeating belief and replacing it with words that will empower you and put you on a path that leads to your desires.

By changing the way you think, power beliefs free you to create the life you want. Because they are so important, they are addressed again in Intention 19.

language from her defeating belief. She replaced it with words that would empower her: "When I get my hopes up, things will work out for me." This became her new power belief.

What defeating beliefs are silently ruling your choices?

Briefcase Moms Balance Zone

The Power of Power Beliefs

Here are some examples of defeating beliefs that have been transformed into power beliefs. Let them inspire you as you identify and deconstruct the beliefs that stand in your way.

Defeating belief: "Decisions I make about my career always end up being mistakes."

Power belief: "Career decisions I make improve my life."

Defeating belief: "If I delegate work, I lose clients."

Power belief: "When I delegate work, my clients are happy and so am I."

Defeating belief: "My daughter prefers her nanny over me."

Power belief: "My daughter and I have a unique relationship."

INTENTION 17—
Weave a Child Care Net

One night as I sat down to unwind in front of the television, I found it wasn't the relaxation I was looking for after a long day. Instead, I was amazed to find myself moved to tears by the program I was watching. It obviously touched a nerve, one of my worst fears as a working mother.

In the television drama, a juvenile court judge was presiding over a case where social services workers wanted to remove two young girls from their single mother's custody. The woman had left her children in the trunk of her car while she was at work.

"Well, really," you might think, "what kind of a crazy person would do that? She deserves to lose her children." But that's not the whole story. It rarely is when we're talking about the competing pulls of committed parenting and demanding careers.

The mother loved and cared for her children deeply. But she was out of options. She had absolutely no one to look after her children and she had to go to work. There were no family members or friends she could turn to. She couldn't leave her young girls at home alone and she could not afford a babysitter. So in her panic she took what she felt was the safest route for her children—she brought them with her. If they were in the trunk, she reasoned, they would be secure. She would know where they were. She checked on the children during her coffee breaks and spent her lunch break with them. She made sure they had toys and were as comfortable as possible. However, when the situation was discovered, the mother was charged with neglect.

As I sat in front of the TV, I was devastated. As much as I recognized this as an extreme case, dramatized for effect, I could identify with the mother's distress and pain. I could follow her logic, which seems crazy from the outside looking in. She was desperate. She felt she had no other child care options. The show was a clear reminder of the chaos we can face as working mothers if we do not build and maintain a first-rate, multipurpose child care net.

Find child care that works for you

If your children are young, one of the most important factors in successfully balancing a career and parenthood is having excellent child care. Many working mothers tell me that knowing their children are safe and thriving while they are at work is the most critical and essential factor in their success. But what makes child care "excellent"? As working parents, we are challenged to consider and reconsider the choices we have made. There are as many studies for as against non-parental child care. Every other month or so I hear or read a media story about the advantages, or the disadvantages, for children of parents sharing the responsibility of full-time child care with child care centers, home daycares, nannies and relatives or friends. If you go looking, you too will likely find studies that both support and criticize your own child care arrangement. It can get pretty confusing.

Of all the working mothers I have spoken with, those who are most at ease with the choices they have made are those who have made their decision based on the individual characteristics of their own child. They are less likely to be bothered by what the "experts" and other individuals (including our own mothers) say is the most appropriate way to care for our children. Remember that even the so-called experts cannot agree on what combination of elements constitutes good mothering or the best child care.

I'll tell you how the sun rose—one ribbon at a time.
— EMILY DICKINSON

By paying attention to your intuition and tuning in to your child or children, you will be less likely to torment yourself about your child care choices, constantly questioning your decision. "Is the child care center too big for my child?" "Does my child spend too many hours in daycare?" "Is being one-on-one with a nanny limiting my child's development?" "Does my child get the appropriate emotional and intellectual stimulation in a home daycare?" "Should I work less and be home more with my children instead of having them cared for by others?" "Would I be happy doing that? How can my partner and I better share child care?" "Is my son spending too much time with my mother?" When you know in your head, in your heart and in your gut that you are doing the right thing *for your child(ren)*, then your child care net can be well woven, no matter what style of care you've chosen.

Arrange basic, premium and disaster coverage

Having excellent child care during the hours that you are working is great. But what about your life after work? Do you have a child care net in place so that you can flourish, too? Is there coverage in place so that you can go out for dinner occasionally or go to a movie? What about that disaster day when your child is too ill to go to the daycare and both you and your spouse are facing critical work deadlines? Is there anyone you can turn to for trusted help? Have you and your partner planned for child care that goes beyond the basic coverage?

"Premium" and "disaster" coverage are not only nice to have, they provide you with peace of mind. This may seem like "just one more thing on the list," such as having that box of earthquake supplies in storage in case of the Big One. But having a plan in place, even if you never need it, will add to your sense of balance as a working mother. You will feel more secure if you have a backup plan.

The extra effort you make to arrange a multipurpose child care net—at a time when you are not desperate—will make all the difference to your sense of calm and control. Making decisions when you are not under duress will also help you to make choices that are best for both you and your children.

Consider flexible and reciprocal child care

There are two things to consider when weaving your child care net—who you can call on and the times you might need additional or emergency child care. Many possibilities exist that you might want to explore. Perhaps there is a drop-in daycare in your neighborhood or near your workplace. Although you might not consider that a great solution for your child on a daily basis, it could provide a backup if your basic coverage falls through. Maybe you have a friend with children with whom you can trade hours for coverage on a Saturday morning when you have a gazillion errands to run. A retired neighbor could occasionally help you out with child care. In exchange you might extend a dinner invitation. Regular play dates can be arranged. Plan a once-a-month sleepover in advance so that you and your partner can go on a "date." See if after-school programs are offered at your children's school that might be available on a part-time or occasional basis. Investigate community resources listed in your local newspaper or on the Internet.

Weaving your child care net might mean reaching out and meeting new people who can become part of your network. You most likely know how to build professional networks, so try using that same approach to ensure that excellent care for your children when you need it most is only a phone call away.

Check Your Balance

There are two things to ponder intentionally in your journal on the topic of child care: how you really feel about your current child care arrangements and how you can weave a child care net without holes. Pull out your journal and write down your thoughts on each of these matters. Try not to judge your comments; just let your pen express your honest thoughts. This way you can discover what is working well and what might need a tune-up.

Here are some more questions to consider.

• How excellent is your current child care situation during the hours that you are at work? During the hours you need for personal time? During emergency

Briefcase Moms Balance Zone
Sane summer schedules

For working mothers with school-age children, summer days are both a blessing and a bother. With children out of school, even the best child care strategies can go awry. The key to keeping your cool is planning, planning and a little more planning.

Community centers, day camps and schools start promoting their "summer" programs in the spring, and in some centers as early as January. Advertisements abound for outdoor swimming lessons, art camps, boating classes, theater retreats and more. Savvy summer survival requires two things: a summer priority list and a calendar.

To ensure you and your family get the most out of your summer fun, write up a list of the things you, your partner and your children would like to do—classes, outings, day camps, sports, vacations. All possibilities go on the list; everyone has a say. Now prioritize that list and star as absolute "must-do's" the top three items you and your partner want to do and the top three items your children want to do. Now that you've determined how each member of the family wants to

times? Remember that "excellence" should be rated on your own personal scale, not some outside valuation.

- Are both your children's and your own needs being met under work, personal and emergency circumstances?

- What would your ideal child care situation look like? If this differs from your current child care net, what changes need to take place?

- Can you identify two steps you can take to create a more disaster-proof child care net?

By analyzing your current situation, you are already closer to creating the child care net you want.

spend their summer, get out the calendar and a highlighter.

First, transfer your and your partner's top three items to the calendar. (Do this in pencil the first time, for you might want to move things around a little.) Now add your children's top three items. Arrange the activities until they feel right to you. Lastly, with this visual view of your ideal summer in front of you, determine what child care arrangements will best support you and your family. Everyone will feel better when they know their needs have been considered.

INTENTION 18—

Remember to Play

Sometimes I ask my clients, "When did you last set aside time to play? When did you last have a laugh-till-your-cheeks-hurt, no-holds-barred good time?" The first response I get is silence. After a few moments most women tell me it's been a long time since they've actually played. It seems that playing tends to take a back seat to more "urgent" things that must be attended to, figured out or taken care of on a daily basis.

When you're searching for balance, however, it is vital to create space for play. Playing restores and re-energizes you. It makes you feel good physically. Play evens out our emotional lives by creating opportunities for us to be not so serious all the time. We just have to look at our children to be reminded of the magical powers of play. Children naturally love to play and innately know how to do it. When children are playing, either individually or in groups, you can see, hear and feel their happiness and contentment—it practically vibrates off them. Children don't think about or analyze it; they just play. Think how that used to feel...playing for the fun of it, for pure pleasure.

I'm making a distinction here between play and fun. Fun is about letting loose and letting go more often. Laughter, silliness, amusement, distraction or nonsense are all elements of fun. Having fun often happens spontaneously; it is often momentary.

Play, on the other hand, is making a conscious decision to forget about the day-to-day pressures of life and work, to enjoy yourself for more than a minute or two, for the sole purpose of pleasure. Play is self-defined. Each of us makes distinct choices about how we play. You may decide that quilting is play for you, while your neighbor's tastes lean toward bungee jumping. Sitting quietly beachside reading a trashy novel might appeal to you as a way to play, to take pleasure in a summer afternoon. Or perhaps an evening of salsa dancing may excite your soul.

Play is something you do just for you, not because it is part of your exercise routine or your home decoration plans. Whatever play is for you, you will know it because it will make you relax and likely make you smile.

Somewhere along the way as we grow up and grow older, we lose our playtime to the responsibilities of adulthood—working hard, being productive, making a difference, looking after others. Yet when you make playing a priority, you can face life, and work, with more enthusiasm and lightness.

> *You* can discover more about a person in an hour of *play than in a year of conversation.*
>
> —PLATO

Connect with your childhood

Some working moms have put play aside for so long they can't remember how to do it any more. Such was the case for Lane, a self-employed management consultant with a ten-year-old son. Here's what she told me.

I've been so busy building my company I haven't had any time for play. All I do is wake up, get my son to school, go to work, pick up my son from after-school care, make dinner, clean up, work late into the evening, go to bed and then get up and do it all over again. In the beginning I didn't mind this pace. It was thrilling for me to watch my business grow. But now I am tired of feeling like all I ever do is work.

My moment of truth came one day while I was waiting for a client to join me for lunch. It was a summer day and I was sitting out on the patio in the warm sunshine. I overheard the conversation at the table next to me where two women about my age were discussing the great time they had on the weekend. They were reminiscing about a group bike ride and barbecue. I felt empty. I couldn't think of the last time I'd done anything like that.

Lane knew she wanted to add a different aspect to her life, but she was not sure how to go about it. We started working together to rediscover and integrate playing into her life. I began by asking her to remember and reflect on the activities she had enjoyed as a child. This would help her to rediscover what play meant to her. It didn't take Lane long to connect with the joys of her childhood. She wrote:

For me it was playing in the woods. I grew up in a house that was at the base of a mountain. There was an orchard directly below it and a forest behind. As a child I would spend hours in the woods finding new trails. When I tapped into that memory, I realized that I would really enjoy hiking—a more grown-up version of playing in the trees. I now make hiking a priority. I go out in the woods at least once a week. I just love it. I always feel terrific after getting out and enjoying nature. My business is still demanding, but it's better balanced with my playtime.

Remembering your childhood loves is a simple way to bring play back into your life. Just indulging in the memories alone will make you feel good.

> *If a man insisted always on being serious, and never allowed himself a bit of fun and relaxation, he would go mad or become unstable without knowing it.*
>
> —HERODOTUS

Have your dessert first

We have come to accept the notion that we must save the best for last. "Eat your vegetables first," we tell our children, "then you can have some cake." Sure, that makes good nutritional sense, but is it necessary all the time? Abandoning routines and shaking it up a little can go a long way to putting a smile on your face. Think of how a child brightens at the prospect of birthday cake in the middle of the afternoon. The same goes with balancing work and play. Sometimes it just makes sense to put play before work.

We are conditioned to think that we must get all our work done before we can give ourselves permission to have a good time. It is as if playing has become the reward for hard work. Playing often seems unavailable to us until...until we've got "everything else" done. But the unfortunate truth for working moms is "everything else" is never done. There is no law that says we have to wait until we've earned the right to play.

Tanis, the mother of a toddler and pregnant with her second child, is a physician floating between a part-time practice and a walk-in clinic. She turned the tables on herself and experimented with playing first and finishing her work later.

> Every weekend it was the same. My husband and I would get up Saturday morning, have a quick breakfast with our

son, check our to-do lists and start running our errands. We'd do things like mow the lawn, buy groceries, clean the gutters, pick up the dry cleaning, clean the windows, put away my son's toys, garden, whatever needed doing. And there's lots that needed doing, that's for sure. By about four in the afternoon, we'd have accomplished most of what we set out to do, but we'd be exhausted. Even if we wanted to do some "fun" stuff, we were too tired.

We decided something had to change. We were spending five days of the week at our businesses and at least one day a week, if not more, just working on or for our house. We agreed to set aside Saturday mornings as our playtime. What a difference this made! We started our weekends playing...the three of us together. We took Brayden to the park one morning and just goofed around in the sand and on the swings. Another Saturday we connected with friends and their children and went out for brunch and to a children's matinee. We still had chores to do, but somehow by playing first they didn't seem so imposing. I think it's because we gained more energy, experienced more pleasure and felt more personal satisfaction. We actually began to look forward to Saturday mornings.

Check Your Balance

Take some time by yourself to think about what playing means to you. To begin with, remember what you loved to do as a child. How did you spend your playtime? If you can't remember, ask a parent or sibling.

In your journal, try to finish the following statements by casting your memory back to a specific occasion. You are trying to tap into some long-ago memories and (let's hope) some not-so-long-ago ones as well. "When I was a child I played..." "The last time I played, I..." Write one full page by finishing either of these statements.

As mentioned, one way to add playtime to your life is to change your routine and do things out of the ordinary. In your journal, recall your last weekend hour by hour. Begin by writing about when you woke up, and write a blow-by-blow description of how you filled up the

Extend *your* weekends by doing the fun stuff first. Try this
and experience a replenishing break from your work routine.

Bring fun to work

While taking time to play is something that usually happens
outside of work, taking moments for fun at work is important,
too. We spend a lot of time there, and even though our
careers may be stimulating, challenging and rewarding, sometimes a little levity is a welcome break. A work environment
that allows for and encourages fun can bring out the best in
people. A workplace that is rigidly and exclusively about work
and only work can stifle creativity, lower morale and increase
absenteeism.

As a manager at a midsize accounting firm, Salma had a
team of ten accountants reporting to her. Every tax season,
she would worry about working the long hours, meeting the
deadlines and keeping her staff motivated. For Salma and her
team this was the most unpleasant time of the year. She wanted
things to be different.

I called a meeting and asked the team what we could do to
make this tax season fun. Well, once everyone got their

day. (If your days off are not weekends, write about the last day off
you had from work.)

Now highlight the time spent
doing chores with a yellow highlighter and the hours spent in
purposeful playtime in blue. This
exercise will show you in living
color whether there's enough downtime in your life. Examine the nature
of the statements highlighted in
blue. Are they things you did at the
end of the day because you were

too exhausted to do anything else?
Does watching reruns of television
sitcoms feature prominently on your
"blue" list? Or are the activities
ones that feed your soul and that
you actively pursue? This analysis
is not about matching up to some
external standard of acceptable
playtime, but rather about recognizing
what your personal needs are and
whether or not they are being met.

heads around the possibility of this tense time of year being enjoyable, the ideas came flying. Where we live the snow is still often on the ground in early spring, so we agreed that converting our office into a Hawaiian haven would lift our spirits through tax time. Everyone got involved. We brought in blow-up palm trees, plastic buckets and pails, and sand. We covered the fluorescent lights with red cellophane and placed beach umbrellas in people's offices. By the time clients started filing returns we had created a tropical, vacation-like atmosphere. We furthered this theme by playing soothing ocean-sound music, hosting the occasional Friday night "Mai Tai" cocktail hour, offering chair massages and playing old beach party movies in the boardroom when people took breaks.

What happened was by letting ourselves have fun at work, tax season felt much less onerous than in years previous. We still had to work hard, but we had a good time, we laughed, we worked better as a team. Even our clients raved about it. It was such a success we are now planning what theme we will have next year.

Making time to play takes more than thinking about it. It takes a commitment. Strengthen your resolve by considering that taking time for play is an age-old dilemma. After all, the familiar statement "All work and no play makes Jack a dull boy" was first written in 1659.

Play is the exultation of the possible.

—MARTIN BUBER

7. Practice

Protection

Safeguard your hopes and protect yourself from injury as you move toward a balanced life. But keep in mind that protection is a two-way street. Although other people can undermine your self-confidence and try to get in the way of your dreams, you can also be your greatest foe. Shield yourself—against believing you're not worth it, against others who might ask too much or try to step over your boundaries, above all against taking on too much, spreading yourself too thin and saying yes too often. Be your own champion.

Intention 19—*Believe You Are Worth It*

Intention 20—*Respect Your Boundaries*

Intention 21—*Rediscover No*

INTENTION 19—

Believe You Are Worth It

Colleen, who has an MBA, runs her own business and is a single mother of two preteen girls, knew that devoting all her waking hours to her work and her children's needs was virtually sucking the life out of her. Although she intellectually saw that taking time for her own interests was, in essence, taking better care of herself, she could not make the leap to really believe in her heart that this was the right thing to do.

In one highly emotional coaching session, Colleen discovered her defeating belief.

> For the first time I realize that I can give 100 percent to my work and to other people, but I do not feel I am worth giving 100 percent to myself. Everyone and everything comes before me. I'm last on my list. I guess, in a way, I think this is the only way to run my life. Each time I've tried to put myself higher up on my own priority list, within a few days or weeks I fall to the bottom again. I feel extremely guilty taking time to do things for me that feel frivolous or selfish. Yet there is a part of me that knows by not believing that I am worth my own time, I am sabotaging myself. I am exhausted. I am impatient with my children and myself. I basically feel completely drained by my business and my kids.

Colleen was held hostage by one of the most invisible yet pervasive defeating beliefs working mothers experience: "I am not worth it."

"I am not worth it" is a quiet thief

When a woman tells me that she doesn't feel she can take time for self-care, that she doesn't feel right about doing something only for herself, that she feels guilty not committing all her time to doing things for others, I know the "I am not worth it" defeating belief is alive and well in her life.

Intention 16, "Blast Away Defeating Beliefs", looks at the role defeating beliefs play in your life and how to blow them up. For working mothers, the "I am not worth it" defeating belief is one of the most debilitating obstacles to living a balanced life. Like an experienced thief, it quietly robs you of your self-confidence, self-esteem and personal power. When you feel unworthy of your own attention, you are much more prone to suffer burnout.

> *You* really have to love yourself to get anything done in this world.
> —Lucille Ball

Once Colleen discovered her "I am not worth it" defeating belief, after her tears dried and her emotions settled down, she began to analyze the life experiences that had led her to create this obstacle in her life.

> I thought to be successful in business I needed to let work take priority in my life. That sacrificing my hobbies, personal interests and social life were the "dues" I had to pay. I felt that I wasn't being a "good" mother if I spent time on me. I believed others' needs, my children and my clients', took precedence over mine. And worst of all I was critical of all that I did. I just never quite measured up in my own eyes.

To construct Colleen's power belief, that she was indeed worth her own consideration, I asked her to look for evidence that was contrary to her current way of thinking. To start with, she was to acknowledge all the things she was great at—she had been focusing on what she "wasn't good enough at" for far too long. I also asked her to look at other successful entrepreneur mothers and study how they were allocating their time. Here is what she discovered.

> I slowly began to acknowledge that I was good at a lot of things, like listening, being loving and loyal, cooking and storytelling. Then I looked around to blast the "bad mother" theory. I took as an example a good friend of mine who's been running her own business for ten years. Natalie runs a very profitable operation and she is what I've always thought to be a very good mother. She has great kids. She takes quarterly weekend spa retreats with her sister and she is part of a weekly running group. This time away from her children seems to only solidify her relationship with them. I started to think maybe this approach could work for me, too.

By seeking out positive role models Colleen was able to see firsthand the personal and professional success other women experience by taking time to nurture themselves and their relationships outside work. Most likely when you first purchased your car, you began to notice others like it everywhere. This heightened awareness applies once you start paying attention to working mothers who believe they are worth it; you'll find these women next door, at work or in your book club.

Check Your Balance

True transformation starts when you understand that you are responsible for your thoughts—positive and negative. Looking inward can be very emotional. So, please give yourself some space and a quiet spot to undertake this balance check.

1. For the next fifteen minutes, ponder the following statements and write down your thoughts and reactions (uncensored) in your journal. Concentrate on one statement at a time and write at least a paragraph on each. First try to recall a specific time when this statement wasn't true and how that affected the way you thought about yourself. Then try to recall a time when this statement *was* true and how that felt.

- I believe I am worthy of my own attention.
- I never criticize myself.
- I regularly recognize and acknowledge my accomplishments.

Give yourself time to re-energize

For a few weeks, Colleen built and fine-tuned this highly personal list of life evidence. Gradually she began to replace her defeating belief with a new power belief. Colleen's power belief became "I am a kind and loving being who is worth the love and attention of others and myself." It was a far cry from her defeating belief that she had articulated so clearly a short time before: "I can give 100 percent to my work and to other people, but I do not feel I am worth giving 100 percent to myself."

Colleen has given herself permission to make room in her life for herself. With a strong intention to change, she has begun to play squash again and she listens to classical music during her commute. She knows this is just a start but the benefits are already beginning to blossom—she has begun to appreciate herself.

Have you heard a critical voice inside your head saying you can't do it, that you don't deserve it or you are not worth it? Do you ever find yourself unconsciously playing second fiddle to everyone else? If so, the "I am not worth it" defeating belief may be influencing your life and it needs to be crushed, now.

- I laugh at my mistakes.
- My thought patterns are healthy and constructive.

2. Review your journal entry. Did you find it easier to recall an instance when the statement was not true than when it was true? Was it difficult to identify generally with these statements? If so, then there's a high probability you are experiencing the "I am not worth it" defeating belief. Now is the time to blast through it.

3. Review Intention 16. Then use your journal to explore ways in which you can eradicate this obstacle from your life path. List the "evidence" supporting this potent defeating belief and replace it with new references that will sustain a new power belief. Take a look at all the wonderful things that make you the person you are. Use this evidence to fuel your belief that you are definitely worth it.

INTENTION 20—

Respect Your Boundaries

W e've all heard of road rage. We've seen or heard the countless media stories detailing how normally mild-mannered individuals completely lose their cool in congested traffic or when another driver cuts them off, and become verbally or physically abusive. It is as if in a single instant a person's anger explodes like a volcano inside the privacy of their car. Rage overtakes all rational thought and behavior. Though you may never have personally experienced road rage, I imagine, if you are completely honest with yourself, that you have experienced something similar—a working mother's rage.

Rage is beyond anger; it is a long way from irritation. It is violent anger with a furious intensity. And it is not pretty. When released it can show up as frustration, foot stomping, raised voices, and the inflicting of physical and emotional pain on others. Rage sends us spiraling downward in the opposite direction of balance.

Not only does rage have a negative impact on the person on the receiving end, but it has a negative impact on the person lashing out as well. No one walks away from rage untouched. Your husband gets home late from the third "Friday night drinks after work" in as many weeks. You've been pacing the floor waiting for him and the minute he steps in the front door, you attack. Angry and hurtful words are exchanged. Your relationship, along with your self-esteem, takes another blow. Your teenager balks once more at his curfew. You feel as if you are constantly enforcing and threatening. Finally, you snap and yell at your son. He yells back and leaves the room, slamming the door behind him. Then you hit bottom. It's a usual pattern that the crescendo of rage is followed by the silent fall into the pit of guilt—regret and remorse for actions taken and words said.

Get off the rage roller coaster

The roller coaster ride of rage is not a pleasant one. The best way to avoid it is not to buy a ticket—to consciously create personal boundaries that clearly articulate what you will let yourself do to others and let others do to you. Boundaries are imaginary lines that surround and protect you and your goals from others. They are also imaginary barriers that dictate your behavior toward others. These invisible borders are self-imposed. You decide what they are to be. You determine what lines you will not allow yourself or others to cross.

Such boundaries will not only protect you from rage— your own and that of others—but will also help you stop putting up with stuff, being taken advantage of and being mistreated by others.

As the executive vice president of marketing for a packaged goods company and mother of twins under four, Bobbi had a very demanding schedule. She was also five months pregnant with her third child. Bobbi was tired and frustrated. She complained that at work she was constantly being asked to stay late for meetings and her hours were getting longer and longer. She was also beginning to feel marginalized at the

Check Your Balance

Boundaries are necessary in all aspects of your life, whether at work or at home, with your children, yourself, your partner or your own parents. Often it's a matter of first articulating them, so that you recognize when they are being crossed. To begin to clarify your boundaries, get out your journal. On one page write the title "How I treat others" and on the opposite page write the title "How others treat me." Under "How I treat others" create three columns: Family, Work, Other Relationships. Under "How others treat me," create the same three columns again. Now list three of the boundaries you have in place in each of those categories on both pages. For example, under "How I treat others," in the Work column, you could note that you do not talk

continued on next page

office. With her maternity leave looming, a couple of her colleagues had begun interrupting her when she spoke in meetings and often dismissed her ideas.

Bobbi was also feeling powerless at home. Her nanny was
regularly late for work. In addition to all this, self-condemnation
was Bobbi's constant companion. She tearfully confessed that
she had been losing her temper frequently with her children.
"I felt anger before I had children, but nothing like the intensity I feel now," she told me. "I would never physically harm
my kids, but I don't even want to be screaming at them either.
I just feel terrible about it all."

Bobbi's lack of personal limits was creating a vicious self-
defeating circle, and she began working with me as her coach
to try to figure out why she was constantly angry. We worked
on strengthening her boundaries. It was obvious to Bobbi that
she needed to use more discipline in dealing with her children,
both for herself and for them. She also discovered that she had
not developed any limits or restrictions as to how others could
treat her. She needed to clarify what she would, and would not,
put up with, and how to communicate these limits to others.

To begin, Bobbi decided to establish some big behavioral
guidelines. She started with her "lines I do not cross" list—

about others behind their backs.
That's a rule you've created for
yourself that sets limits on your
personal behavior. Under the Family
column, you might write that you
do not allow your children to insult
you. Identify whether each of these
are strong or weak boundaries.
Next determine one new boundary
in each category that would make
your life easier. Add it to the
relevant column.

Boundaries that govern your
own behavior are often easier to
strengthen than those that govern
how others treat you. So work on
the easier ones first. Note which
personal restrictions you wish to
strengthen, and make a commitment to yourself to work on these
over the next month. This can be as
broad as identifying what kind of a
person you want to be, and be seen
as, or as specific as committing not

rules that dictated how she would allow herself to act. Knowing that she was the only one who could control how she reacted to situations, she pledged to embrace the following: "I will not yell at my children. I will not swear in front of my children. I will not respond to my children if I am in a rage. I will give myself a time-out when I am in a rage. I will treat others with respect." Next, she created a list of restrictions that set out the kind of behavior she would accept from others: no raised voices, no sarcasm, no condescending tones, no unsolicited criticism, no tardiness and no offensive language.

Bobbi was keen to start implementing her new boundaries. She was ready to police her own actions and ready to educate others about her standards. She just wasn't sure how to go about it.

Protect your boundaries gracefully

I shared with Bobbi a way for herself and others to respect her boundaries. This seven-step process, keyed to the acronym RESPECT, works every time. The statements below in parentheses are self-talk you can use through this process, and the words in quotation marks are examples of language you

to swear or not to be late. When reviewing the boundaries that dictate what you view as acceptable treatment by others, note which ones you've communicated clearly to others and which you have not. Boundaries won't work if people don't know they are there. Figure out whom you need to tell, and don't be afraid to start talking if the limits you have identified for yourself are crossed. At the least, this will allow you to explain your boundaries and educate others about what appropriate conduct means to you.

can use to communicate with others. When you are communicating your boundaries, ensure you start the conversation with your voice completely devoid of any emotion. The tone of voice you use should be similar to how you sound when making a comment on the weather—calm and confident.

R   Recognize your boundaries are being crossed. Stop yourself and/or others just as you/they start to cross the line. (I am violating my personal boundary.) "Excuse me."

E   Educate yourself and/or others that they are violating your boundary. (I am starting to raise my voice.) "Do you realize you are yelling at me?"

S   Stop. Stop your behavior and/or request that others stop. (Stop this action right now.) "I'd like you to stop yelling at me."

P   Promote. Tell yourself and/or others how your limits can be respected. (I need to pause and think before I speak or react.) "Please speak to me calmly."

E   Embrace yourself and/or others for cooperating. (Congratulations, self. I kept my cool and respected my own behavior code.) "Thank you for respecting my wishes."

C   Command that you/they stop. (I must stop yelling.) "I insist that you stop raising your voice to me." If nothing changes, then call it quits.

T   Take off. Leave the situation. (I can't control my emotions right now. I must leave the situation and cool off, alone.) "I can't have this conversation while you are yelling at me. I am going to leave the room. Let's talk about this when we are not as upset."

In most cases, if you've reached Step 5 (Embrace) in the process you will have policed yourself and kept your boundaries intact. If not, then the last two steps will put things in order. Also, if others are not cooperative and are still crossing your boundaries, the final two steps will resolve the situation (at least for the present). Rarely do these final steps have to come into play. In most cases, you and others will change behavior after Step 2 (Educate).

Bobbi got great results at home using this method. By clearly communicating her boundaries, she was able to reduce her frustration with her children. Although at first she found it a bit more awkward to set limits at work and with her nanny, the confidence she gained trying it out with her children gradually made that easier, too. She set restrictions on her workday and abided by them by saying no to certain requests (see Intention 21 for more details). Her relationships with co-workers improved slowly as she became more able to assert her opinion and request the space to say what she felt was valid. She had a long talk with her nanny and came to a new agreement on work hours that they both could live with. And most importantly, from Bobbi's perspective, she learned to be more patient with herself. "I still get upset with my children, but I haven't raised my voice to them in weeks," she told me a couple of months after establishing her boundaries. "I've had a few close calls, but I've been able to discipline myself now that I know exactly what my limits are. And I do feel a lot better about myself."

Not all situations resolve as quickly or as positively as Bobbi's. If you have been operating without personal limits for a long while, you will need time to create and consistently respect your boundaries. Go easy on yourself; you will get there. In some cases, people won't comply with these limits even after you ask them to. Remember, you are on a journey to live a balanced life without guilt and stress. You might have to walk away from some individuals and situations...and let go of things that don't work for you. When you take the time to define and strengthen your boundaries, you will find yourself in a generally happier and calmer state.

INTENTION 21—

Redisover No

In its simplest terms, balance is really a two-letter word—
no. Without the word no, balance cannot exist.

No is such a strong word. There is a sense of control that comes with voicing those letters N-O. I think that's why children say no so frequently and forcefully (at least my child does). It just feels good. Children know what they like or don't like and they are not afraid to tell you.

So here's the question: If saying no came naturally to us as children, when did we unlearn the ability? Why do we, as career-oriented moms, subordinate our preferences to the point that we have real trouble saying no to the things we don't want to do?

If you don't think you are worth it (see Intention 19), you will find it very difficult to muster the courage to stand up for yourself and say no. With nonexistent or weak boundaries in your life and relationships, you will find it extremely challenging to protect your own interests. And sometimes, saying no is plain tough because it feels uncomfortable. Many working moms have told me they have been socialized to be accommodating, so turning down an offer or declining an invitation can induce feelings of shame or worry. You say yes to organizing the school sports fundraiser or canvasing door-to-door, even though you know your time is already stretched very thin. You are concerned you might annoy or lose some of the people close to you by saying thanks, but no. If you turn down a request from a co-worker, you wonder if you are compromising your advancement or damaging your professional relationship.

Say no with confidence

Saying no is a skill that can be rediscovered. Part of you still remembers how to do it; you may just be out of practice. Perhaps reacquainting yourself with some techniques that will raise your comfort and confidence is in order. Your ability to say no with confidence will protect you from engaging in obligations and opportunities that do not reflect what is important to you. And being able to gracefully refuse requests will safeguard you from feeling taken advantage of and burnt out.

> *I have discovered in life that I can do anything, but I can't do everything.*
> —ROBERT SCHULLER

Whether you want to say no on the personal or professional front, here are five steps to make it easier for you.

Focus on your priorities

Practice saying no to everything that is not on your priority list. In doing so you will be honoring your deepest desires. Start with the easy stuff first. Turn down something you really don't want to go to or do—your local homeowners' annual get-together, the seventh soccer game in a row in the rain, an early breakfast meeting. It may feel like you are sticking needles in your eyes at first, but the more you experiment with saying no, the easier it will become.

One of the most powerful tools you can use in getting to "no" is to ask yourself the following questions: *Whatever I am saying yes to, what am I saying no to? Whatever I am saying no to, what am I saying yes to?* For example, by saying yes to that breakfast meeting, are you saying no to an early morning snuggle with your toddler? By saying no to that weekend assignment, can you still say yes to attending your son's out-of-town hockey tournament? These simple questions should put options in perspective and help you say yes to your priorities.

Grasp all, lose all.
—Fourteenth-century proverb

Discover your fears

Fear often gets in the way of saying no to people or commitments in our life. For example, some working moms find saying no in their professional life more challenging than in their personal life. Asserting yourself at the office can feel far more vulnerable. The perceived or imagined consequences of saying no to your boss, clients or colleagues can stop you from claiming that right, because you feel your livelihood is at stake. When you identify the source of your fear, you can develop a strategy to confront it head-on. This worked for Harsha, executive director for a not-for-profit agency and mother of three, when she found herself volunteering for yet another marketing committee at work.

> Even as my voice was saying yes to this commitment, my mind was screaming no. I wanted to say no when they asked me, but I was afraid to. I just felt that if I didn't take on this role, I'd be sending a message to my board that I was uncooperative...
>
> Yet I knew my inability to refuse requests at work was compromising my physical and mental health. By saying yes to everything that was thrown at me, I was compromising my needs and my self-esteem. When I realized that fear (of losing my job) was causing me to take on more than I could handle, I began to examine that fear. When I weighed the risks of no job versus a stressed-out and unhealthy me, I

was finally motivated to start balancing my work-related decisions with saying yes to what I value.

I took some calculated risks, which fortunately worked out well for me. I said no to staying late one night and re-negotiated my involvement in the marketing committee. I am no longer chair and need only attend meetings once a month, instead of weekly. Saying no has become a freeing experience for me. Now my days are filled with less regret and resentment. I have also discovered that saying no has not caused me to offend anyone or lose my job. In fact, it has had the opposite effect. By clearly communicating my boundaries and preferences, I have gained more respect from colleagues, board members and clients. I no longer feel like a pushover.

Deconstructing a situation in which you are fearful of saying no often minimizes or eliminates the fear itself—and makes saying no much easier.

> *Saying no can be the ultimate self-care.*
> —CLAUDIA BLACK

Give people advance notice

Let people in your life know that you intend to honor your new priorities and that you will be saying no more often. This pre-pares both you and them for your new behavior. Your friends will better accept you declining weekend invitations if you explain in advance that Sundays are family days. People in your work world will find it easier to accept your new way of doing things if you give them advance notice. You could explain dur-ing your performance review or team meetings that you will be delegating certain kinds of work and changing your hours for more flexibility. However, don't be surprised if the first few times you decline a request, you get a stunned or shocked response. Keep at it; consistency is the key. And don't forget that saying no to someone or something else means saying yes to you.

Imagine the possibilities

If you could say no to something you are currently doing, knowing that there would be absolutely no hard feelings or negative consequences, what would you say no to? This question is a real eye-opener, and your answers may go beyond your priority list. Sometimes, when we are developing priority lists, the most obvious things rise to the surface first. When you delve deeper and really question what else you could let go of, the answers can be interesting. If you discover a new priority, add it to your list.

Stand up for yourself

How effective you are at saying no will depend on how you communicate your stance to others. Saying no is like communicating a boundary. The body language you employ and the voice you use need to be neutral. Others will find it easier to accept a negative response if it is said in a respectful manner.

Check Your Balance

Open your journal and get ready for some brainstorming. Ponder the following questions, without writing anything down. Just let your initial reactions wash over you.

- Do I feel comfortable saying no at the office?
- When do I feel most comfortable saying no?
- When do I feel least comfortable saying no?
- What am I saying yes to that I would much prefer not to be doing?
- What do I want to say no to that I am currently saying yes to out of habit or obligation?
- Is there a simple thing I can do to feel more comfortable saying no?
- How do I protect myself from unexpected requests for my time and energy?
- Who do I need to be saying no to?
- Am I clear on what my real priorities are?
- What steps do I need to take to start saying no to things that are not priorities for me?

Use clear language and hold your position. Even when you are clearly saying no to someone, sometimes they are not willing to accept the response. They may continue to ask in other ways or outright cajole you into accepting. Be fair and firm; stand your ground and repeat your response. Eventually your message will be heard.

This worked for Lindsey, mom of eight- and five-year-old boys and senior partner in a national tax firm, when she approached a project she had done for the past four years in a very different way.

> Every year at Christmas, my children's school has a turkey lunch for the entire school (think turkey dinner for 400 people). The teachers cook the turkeys, one mom cooks up 100 boxes of stuffing, and a parent volunteer organizes all the rest. For the past four years I have been that volunteer. The first year I did it, I had very little guidance from the previous organizer and ended up doing everything myself. The second year, I again thought I had to do everything and ended up with a serious back injury. Last year, I split up the tasks with another mom who was working at home and could help with a lot of the preliminary running around. This year I agreed to do it again, but I made it very clear

- What is the worst thing that could happen if I say no at work? at home?
- What is the best thing that could happen if I start saying no?
  Now spend fifteen minutes writing an "action" list of things you want to say no to first, such as unreasonable overtime, grocery shopping or another extended family event. This list is intended to move you closer to being able to say no to things you choose not to do or which are not important to you. In doing this, it should bring you closer to the real priorities in your life. Your action list may be oriented toward work, household chores or relationships. Any one of these is a good area in which to begin saying no. Start by choosing three specific activities that are draining your time. Then commit to saying no to each one for the next two weeks. When those weeks have passed, pause and measure what you have gained by saying no.

from the start what I would and would not do. I would do the organizing but someone else had to order the turkeys, get them delivered to the school and pick up all of the supplies.

It sure was a different feeling not having my hands in everything, but I am proud of myself for sticking to my original plan and saying no to the tasks I just knew I didn't want to do again. Now that I have let someone else help with the organizing of the turkey lunch and we have a detailed list of what has to be done, my plan is to let someone else take over completely. I will of course volunteer to help on the day of the lunch.

It has taken some time to feel comfortable saying no and delegating these tasks to someone else, but it has kept my stress level certainly lower as I try to deal with all of the other demands at that particular time of the year.

Rediscover the power of no to balance your life. Saying no with confidence and care will not alienate you from others; instead it will bring you new-found energy, space and respect.

Briefcase Moms Balance Zone

Ten reasons to say no

1. To recover lost time
2. To focus on your priorities
3. To have more fun
4. Because it feels good
5. To bolster your self-esteem
6. To do what you really want to do
7. To let go of draining situations or people
8. Because you really want to
9. To create some space in your life
10. To gain respect from others

8. Practice

Connection

The key to balanced living is figuring out how to strengthen the connection between the way you live your life now and your vision of what you want your life to be. Examining what's bothering you can lead to creating your vision of balance. Reaching your vision is seldom a solitary effort, and often it is more successful when you have support along the way. Forming heartfelt, soulful connections with those who travel with you makes for a joyous shared experience. Making the connections between everything you do and everyone you touch will ensure you resist the temptation to go it alone.

Intention 22—*Transform Complaints into a Vision*

Intention 23—*Create a Sisterhood of Support*

Intention 24—*Build Powerful Relationships*

INTENTION 22—

Transform Complaints into a Vision

We all have good days and bad days. On our good days life seems to flow. You are on time for all your appointments, your children are in good health, and you and your partner are in sync. You feel you're heading in the right direction in your life and everything seems manageable. Then there are the bad days. Things are piling up around you, traffic is snarled, and arguments explode within your family. The grocery bag breaks and you can't find your car keys. These are the days you find yourself full of complaints.

If anyone were to ask how you were and expect a real answer, as opposed to the one-word "Fine" that you normally deliver, you might say, "I feel overwhelmed and overcommitted. Every hour of my week is scheduled. I don't have a sense of purpose. I'm so tired. My responsibilities to my work, children, community and partner are all clamoring for my attention. I don't have time to exercise. I rarely have fun." On these days you'd probably also find yourself thinking, "How can I better balance my work and family life?"

The answer depends on you. There is no one right or wrong way to live a balanced life—only your way. Many of us fall into the trap of thinking that there is some universal method of living well. There isn't. And then we add to our stress by thinking our lives would be less chaotic and more fulfilling if we followed someone else's lead. Your colleague does flextime; maybe that's the answer for you. Your neighbor has a nanny to take care of her children during the day; possibly you should have one, too. Your friend runs her own business; that seems like a workable solution. Your anxiety level rises as you continue to question your own choices. This kind of self-doubt and self-torture is common when you are managing life as a working mom without a clear vision of what balanced living means to you.

Creating a personal "balance vision"—your dream picture of a life that both nurtures you and looks after your family—enables you to visualize your future. Your balance vision is open-ended and arises from your internal perspective of what you believe is possible for your life. It focuses on only one aspect of your overall personal vision, the one that questions how you are going to juggle your various responsibilities and desires while ensuring your personal equilibrium. (You can create visions for other aspects of your life as well—career, education, recreation, relationships, volunteering, and so on. Let's stick with the balance vision for now.) The purpose of your balance vision is very specific: to provide a clear picture of your ideal work-life balance. If well crafted, it will inspire you to live the life you want.

> *Start by doing what is necessary, then what is possible, and suddenly you are doing the impossible.*
>
> —SAINT FRANCIS OF ASSISI

Simply put, your balance vision gives you a destination. It gives you something to strive for and to work toward. It will pull you forward even if you are having a less than stellar day. And as the old saying goes, if you know where you are going, it is much easier to get there.

Moving from theory to practice

This sounds good in theory. But how do you create a practical balance vision that is both inspiring and reachable? The easiest way is to start paying attention to what you are complaining about. Embedded in your complaints are your priorities... and a balance vision must be rooted in your priorities.

For eight years, Melissa had been self-employed, running her own one-person public relations business. It was only after she began to analyze her complaints and to find patterns emerging in her conversations with others that she was able to put her grievances to good use. She created her balance vision.

My job is exciting and rewarding, but also very demanding. I am a highly organized person, but the nature of my business means I never know from one day to the next what I might be up against. I do a lot of work in crisis communications, so when my clients face an emergency I have to drop everything and be ready to fly into action. I was able to manage this frenetic pace quite well until I had my first child. After Ben was born, I started to resent the erratic hours. I felt the demands of my job were compromising my time with my son. I was also beginning to question being in business for myself. I felt like I was putting a lot of time and energy into the business but I didn't feel like I was getting much in return. I realize now that I was constantly complaining to anyone who would listen that I never had enough time for Ben, that my clients had no respect for my personal schedule, that my friendships were suffering, that my husband and I never saw each other any more, that I was constantly feeling tired.

What I was complaining about was really a request in disguise to honor a priority that my heart was aware of but not necessarily my head. By more clearly articulating my priorities around work-life balance, I really was able to pull together the words to describe a vision for my family and me. By listening carefully to myself and paying close attention to the words that I poured into my journal, I solidified a balance vision. As it turned out, for me, a balanced life right now is to work four days a week focusing on strategic communications planning with a core set of clients that respect my commitment to their success and mine. Having gone that far, I needed to figure out how to achieve this vision. I came up with three clear points: reorient my business around a few core clients who respect and honor my commitment to them but also to myself; change the nature of my business to focus on strategic planning rather than crisis communications, which would give me more control over my response time; and limit my working hours to four days a week so that I would have more time with my son, my husband and friends. This last point was probably the biggest change and the most surprising after eight years of building up the business. It is not perfect yet, but I feel I am making progress. I feel I'm on the right path.

A personal balance vision will motivate you and pull you forward by creating a vacuum between where you are in your life right now and where you want to go. When your vision is clear, the steps toward your future become obvious and feel much easier to undertake.

> *Our* willingness to create a new dream or vision for
> ourselves is a statement of belief in our own potential.
>
> —David McNally

Check Your Balance

Developing your balance vision means giving yourself permission to wish for what could be possible in your life. To get started, jot down in your journal all the things you find yourself complaining about. Take about fifteen minutes to list whatever comes to mind. (You may wish to revisit this exercise as your week progresses. You may not even be aware right now that you're complaining about certain aspects of your life.) Review this list and examine each complaint, looking for a request that might be hidden under the surface. For example, if a complaint is "I never have any time to myself," the request most likely is "I want to have time alone." When you uncover the request underneath the complaint, you've begun the process of identifying your priorities.

continued on next page

Update your balance vision

Defining a balance vision is the first step. Keeping your balance is the second. It requires flexibility and awareness and an acknowledgment of the effect changes in your life will undoubtedly have on your vision. Real balance is fluid; it changes when we do. A tightrope walker does not lean to one side all the way across the Big Top. You too have to correct and alter your position all along the way.

A new job, a baby, divorce, a death—all these major life events will have an impact on your balance vision. So every six months or so, particularly when your children are small and changes happen so quickly, assess your circumstances and reflect on your vision. Determine whether it is still applicable or whether you need to alter it slightly to accommodate new circumstances in your life. Perhaps the vision remains valid, but how you go about achieving it might need a tune-up. If you have put an honest effort into creating your vision, it will likely remain true. However, the path you follow to reach your vision may require modifications over the years, as you age and as your children grow.

A sense of peace comes with having a balance vision. You

Narrow down the list to your top five priorities and write them on a separate page.

Next do a little brainstorming by letting your mind consider the following questions. Don't try to answer them yet. Just allow yourself to ponder them.

- What is my ideal work-life balance right now?
- What might have changed five years from now?
- How many hours a week (or days a week) do I want to work?
- How many vacations a year do I want?
- What kind of work do I love to do?
- How much money do I need?
- What will I do with this money?
- What will I do with my free time?
- What would be an ideal environment in which I could do my best work?
- What are the type of people and the resources I need to do my best work?

know that each day you are moving toward living your life the way you intend. You may not be there yet, but you know where "there" is. You are living with intention. You are following your own agenda—not the agenda of society, your parents, your partner, your colleagues or your friends. And with time, persistence and dedication, you will arrive at your chosen destination.

Briefcase Moms Balance Zone
Balance visions that work

Below are samples of my clients' balance visions to spark your imagination. Each balance vision is as unique as the person who created it.

- "Working four days a week at the office—three days from 8:30 to 5:30, and one day from 8:30 to 8:30. My day off is split evenly between time with my children and time for myself. My weekends are dedicated family time. I take four vacations a year—one alone, one with my husband and two as a family."

- How much time a week do I want to spend with my children? my partner?
- How much time a week do I want to spend alone?

  After considering these questions, in your journal, write a balance vision statement that reflects both your priorities and the thoughts that have arisen as you contemplated the questions above. "For me, a balanced life is..."

  The simpler the language, the stronger the balance vision. Do your best to keep it to a maximum of thirty-five words. Remember, you're not committed to this vision forever just by writing it down today, and you might write something entirely different tomorrow. A strong vision takes time to develop. The key here is to not allow any tendency toward perfectionism to keep you from putting pen to paper. Write something... it's a beginning. Keep it open for all possibilities without censorship. Just let the vision take shape.

• "Continue to take on consulting contracts, which allows me to be at home with my children and work while they are in school and in the evenings after they have gone to bed. Take the summers off work and spend them with my children. Have a weekly 'date' with my husband and dedicate one afternoon a week to my self-care."

• "Be promoted in one year and advance my salary by 15 percent. Work full-time with an aim to restructure my hours to 9:00 a.m. to 3:00 p.m. in three years, when my youngest child is in elementary school. Take two weeks' holiday every Christmas and two weeks in the summer."

Vision without action is a daydream. Action without vision is a nightmare.

—JAPANESE PROVERB

INTENTION 23—

Create a Sisterhood of Support

Much of this book is about building more support in our lives. Earlier intentions looked at different kinds of communities of support—workplace teams, partners in parenting and your child care safety net. Some of us may have these support systems firmly in place, while others are working toward establishing them. No matter what stage you are at in this process, choosing to consciously create these communities is critical to your balance and will enable you to experience a richer and more joyful life. However, they can neither replace nor fill a working mother's deep longing for heartfelt, soulful connections with friends.

This intention focuses on friendships outside of the primary relationship you may have with your spouse or partner. Because they involve a unique set of demands and expectations, these friendships have a different sensibility than the marriage or life partnership. (For more on being with your partner, see Intentions 2, 14 and 26.) It also focuses on the relationships we form with other women, more so than men. Not to say male friendships aren't just as important. But they are special in their own way.

Our true friendships are often our most cherished connections. With our friends we are most comfortable sharing our real selves—free to be who we really are and who we are becoming. With our closest companions we feel safe to express and exchange our truths, to make mistakes, to be silly or sad and laugh or cry till it hurts. Friends touch our lives in many different ways. Friends make us who we are. They keep us grounded and honest and let us blow off steam. They teach us things and continually open our hearts. The impact of a good friendship can be fleeting—a hug on a bad day—or lifelong— words of wisdom that forever guide our decisions. The women who are dearest to us are the connective fabric of our lives.

> *Each* friend represents a world in us, a world possibly not born until they arrive.
>
> —Anaïs Nin

Friendships combat loneliness

Although surrounded by people (sometimes it feels like every waking moment of the day), many of us feel lonely and isolated. We crave time alone, yet at the same time we yearn for the deeper connection of sisterly love. We seek to be understood and to understand. We want to share stories with someone we trust who empathizes with our situation. Without the loving care that is the heart of a solid friendship, we experience a sense of emptiness and loss in our lives.

This is exactly how I felt a few years ago. I was engrossed in the building of my public relations consulting firm. I let it consume me. My life became my business. I put off calling my girlfriends because I was too busy. I hadn't talked to many of them in such a long while that I knew any phone call I made would demand at least a forty-five-minute conversation. And I definitely didn't have that kind of time, or so I thought. Sometimes I would send an e-mail. Or maybe I would call when I knew they weren't going to be there so that I could simply leave a message. Many times I did nothing. My social networks invited me to lunch or to parties and I'd often decline, choosing to work instead. Of course, over time my friendships began to unravel. After an intense week of work, I'd find myself on a Friday afternoon with no weekend plans and no one to talk to who wasn't connected with my work.

Nobody sees a flower—really—it is so small it takes time—we haven't time—and to see takes time, like to have a friend takes time.

—GEORGIA O'KEEFFE

Check Your Balance

Creating and maintaining friendships is an investment in our well-being. We like to be around people who make us feel good. We can also learn a lot from relationships that challenge and stretch us. There is a fine line, however, between relationships that help us grow and those that drain us. Our true friends are there to celebrate our successes and see us through our tough times. You will benefit from clarifying which relationships in your life sustain you and which do not. It also helps to know what kind of friend you are and the impact you are having on the lives of others. Take fifteen minutes to contemplate these questions.

• What does being a friend mean to me?

• Am I a good friend to others?

• What expectations do I have of my friends? Do I rely too heavily on some friends?

Through coaching others I have since found that my situation was not unique. Because of the daily pressures of our lives, it can be challenging to make the time and create the mental space needed to develop and maintain friendships. These precious relationships can take a back seat to other priorities, subconsciously or consciously. If you are maxed out with work and raising children, finding the time to establish high-quality relationships with others can be difficult. If you've just relocated to a new city, making new friends can be formidable and extremely time-consuming. If your job demands a lot of travel, staying in contact with close companions and attending social events can be a challenge. Yet truly connecting with our girlfriends is essential to a life of balance.

Friendships reduce stress

We know how good we feel after talking with a friend. When women are stressed and upset—about health concerns, relationship problems or work-related conflicts—we tend to reach out to a friend. Even if no solutions have been found, just that sense of connection, of naming the concern, is helpful. Friends allow us to release our worries and fears in safety. The positive

- Who are my friends now? What qualities do they have and why are they my friends?
- Who do I want to see more of? Whose company do I enjoy the most?
- Who lifts me up and inspires me? Who do I want to get to know better?
- What friendships need improving? What conversations do I need to have to repair or enhance an existing friendship?

- Is there a particular person in my life to whom I could be a better friend? How?
- Who zaps my energy? Who takes up too much of my time?
- Are there friendships that I need to let go of? Can I imagine myself doing that?
- In viewing my friends as a mirror of me and my life, what do I see?
- What changes do I need to make to surround myself with a community of connection?

continued on next page

impact friendships have on our emotional health was borne out in a research study done by psychologist Shelley Taylor of the University of California, Los Angeles, in 2000. The study revealed a pattern of responding to stress she termed "tend-and-befriend." She maintains that female stress responses have evolved for the protection of offspring and involve affiliation with social groups, especially networks of females.

In her study, Taylor points out that this stress response is seen in many species. Females respond to stressful conditions by protecting and nurturing their young (the "tend" response) and by seeking social contact and support from others—especially other females (the "befriend" response). Befriending methods in our North American culture include talking on the phone with relatives or friends, or even such simple social contacts as asking for directions when we're lost. When we are stressed, essentially, women prefer to be with others, especially other women.

Some friendships are time based, and others are soul based. Friends can be made at certain periods in your life—your friends from school, friends from the neighborhood in which you grew up, the friends you made at college and most of the friends you make at work. Then there are those friends

Once you have reflected on these questions, take five minutes to write down in your journal whatever comes to mind about one particular friend in your life. Just let your thoughts flow, as you have learned to do throughout this book.

Take another five minutes and repeat this exercise, concentrating on another person in your life whom you consider your friend.

As you reread what you've written, make three specific promises to yourself to alter or reorient your friendships based on your discoveries. Write down these commitments. Following through may not be easy. You may have to reach out and make new connections, repair damaged friendships or let go of some draining relationships. Making the changes will take effort, honesty and dedication on your part, but isn't that what friendship is all about?

with whom you feel a bond that transcends time. Your circle of friends will be unique to you; there are no set rules around a magic number of friends. Rather, it is a very individual choice as to the quality—the level of trust, communication and love in a relationship—and the quantity of friendships you want to share. You may be completely satisfied with one close friend that you can talk to during your workday. You may rely on your childhood friend to keep you in touch with your past, and you may draw close other friends you've made through your children's school activities and with whom you discuss parenting issues. Or you may enjoy being surrounded by lots of people, all of you sharing and participating. Whatever the combination, the right fit is one that energizes you and enables you to offer and accept loving connection.

When I realized that I had been compromising my ability to maintain and make friends, I consciously chose to make people my priority. I began with a commitment to myself to create community. I made it my overriding intention to build more solid, intimate connections. I did an about-face regarding the time and attention I put into this aspect of my life. I began to nurture my friendships like a garden. I watered. I weeded. I planted. I intentionally put myself out there to meet new people, to spend time with old friends and re-establish lost connections. I oriented my free time around supporting and being with those close to me. I stopped putting my work ahead of the people in my life. I let go of relationships that were no longer mutually emotionally beneficial. When I changed my focus, I began to slowly reap the rewards. It took time and it took a reorientation to better balance. But today I have a strong network of friends that I share, care, cry and laugh with, and my life is richer for that.

INTENTION 24—

Build Powerful Relationships

As Albert Schweitzer received the Nobel Prize in 1952, he acknowledged his sense of community when he said, "You don't live in a world all alone. Your brothers are here too." Few who accomplish great things do it without the contributions of others. Other people encourage and support them along the way. And the same goes for the rest of us, who may not win the Nobel.

Of course, you *can* go it alone. Many working mothers try, and a few are successful at it. But I've found that those women who collaborate with others achieve success with more ease and more grace. Taking the time to build powerful relationships is a basic component of a balanced life. The support and synergy you will experience as you create mutually beneficial partnerships, especially in your professional life, will catapult you forward in your career...and you'll have more fun succeeding than you would on your own.

When Hillary, a senior vice president of business development for a clothing manufacturer and mother of a ten-year-old daughter and six-year-old son, fell victim to an unexpected downsizing, she realized that her self-imposed extreme independence had left her isolated and scrambling.

I always prided myself on my ability to do things "on my own." I've always been the kind of person who enjoyed my own company. Oh sure, I'd heard the theory of the benefits of having a strong network, but I didn't think it applied so much to me. Also, the thought of making small talk at networking events and handing out business cards just didn't appeal. I now realize that deep down I did not believe that others could, or would, really help me. I'd achieved a successful career by myself through hard work and high performance. And I would have continued thinking that way had I not been laid off when my department was suddenly "restructured."

After my head stopped reeling and I came to terms with the fact that I was unemployed, I suddenly realized that I had no one to turn to for professional support. I wouldn't say I fell into a depression, but I did feel completely isolated and, for the first time in my life, started to question my "lone ranger" style. More importantly, I had to figure out a way to start building a professional and personal network, and that scared me because I had no idea where or how to get started.

Hillary saw that her belief that networking was a superficial practice had limited her ability to form positive, jointly supportive professional relationships. By looking at building relationships from a different viewpoint—seeing the power and the reward in partnerships—she was able to begin creating her own personal support team.

> *The key* is to keep company with people who uplift you, whose presence calls forth your best.
> —ELIZABETH WILLETT

Find a success partner

A "success partnership" is a relationship, based on mutual respect, accountability and commitment, with someone you trust and feel comfortable with. Each partner supports the other to reach their goals. After much consideration and encouragement, Hillary plucked up her courage and asked a former colleague, Sharon, if she'd be interested in teaming up with her. To Hillary's surprise, Sharon was enthusiastic about the chance to form a success partnership. She'd always admired Hillary, albeit from afar, and she, too, as a result of the company's downsizing, had taken on a task that was new to her. Sharon was about to organize a management seminar for her company and was excited about the prospect of one-to-one support to move her own plans along.

The two agreed to support each other for three months. Sharon committed to help Hillary in her job search, and Hillary agreed to help Sharon stay on track with her seminar planning. They set up regular weekly telephone meetings to report their progress and encourage each other to take new steps. The systematic reciprocal support meant Hillary kept focused and motivated in looking for a new position and Sharon's project was well managed and never became out-of-control.

Create an inner circle

An inner circle is not as structured as a success partnership. But surrounding yourself with people you can rely on and who are invested in supporting you to be your best can be just as effective. Most of us have an inner circle—we just don't realize it. Those individuals closest to us, such as our life partner, a favorite aunt, a dear friend, a close colleague, a mentor or coach can form the nucleus of an effective inner circle.

Check Your Balance

What is your relationship style? Have you created a personal support team (although you may not have called it that)? Do you have people in your life who are actively engaged in helping you reach your goals, or do you prefer to go solo? To find out, consider the following statements, then use your reaction to them as a catalyst for some personal journal time. Read the statements first, sit with your reactions for two minutes, then write without stopping for five minutes. Let your thoughts flow without consciously editing them as you write.

- Powerful people don't need help to be successful.
- I have never really considered getting support or collaboration from others.
- I don't share my plans with others because if I fail I don't want them to know.

Although in the past Hillary had made little time for relationships outside of her family, she was delighted to discover that she did have five people she could consider to be in her inner circle. She decided to ease up on her need to be fully independent and let these people into her life in a much more open and collaborative manner than she had in the past.

For Hillary, this was a big step, for she had worked hard to project an image of a strong, independent woman. She started slowly by sharing her fears, frustrations and dreams with each of them over the course of several weeks. She told them about her embarrassment at being out of work and her uncertainty about her ability to find a similar position again. And they reciprocated by providing a different perspective and often giving her valuable insight.

Build smart connections

Soon Hillary was ready to branch out further and start forming "smart connections." A smart connection is like a strategic alliance between companies, but on a personal level. Both types of alliances, if properly managed, create shared success for all involved. A smart connection is formed when one person

- Building a personal support team takes a lot of time.
- I like helping other people solve their problems.
- Relationships work best if I get as much as I give.
- I don't ask people to support me because I am afraid they will say no or think I don't know what I'm doing.

Once you've determined your relationship style, think about where you could most use support in your life. Can you identify people or groups that could make a difference? In your journal, write down one area you have identified where you could use more support. Then make a note of three people or groups of people that might make a difference.

Perhaps you already have a support network. If so, in your journal, write one page assessing its effectiveness and relevance. Is it meeting your

continued on next page

exchanges her skills, knowledge, services or connections (in other words, her "smarts") with another. Working mothers are particularly adept at forming smart connections. Think of all the exchanges you do naturally with friends, acquaintances and colleagues. You work Monday through Friday with Thursdays off, while your co-worker works full-time. You transport her daughter to art class on Thursday mornings with your daughter and return her to daycare later in the day. In exchange, your co-worker hosts a play date at her house on Saturday afternoons so you can run errands. Your best friend is an avid book buyer and you're a movie junkie. She lends you books and you advise her on movies to see. You can have as many smart connections as you want, each helping you in a multitude of ways. They can run for a set period of time or indefinitely. Smart connection partners increase your balance by providing you with leverage, advice and support.

The beauty of smart connections is that they are not limited to one-to-one relationships. You can form a smart connection with a group of like-minded individuals. Just as CEOs have boards of directors and many small-business owners have advisory boards, you, too, can create your own group to support you professionally. You can brainstorm and share skills with a special collection of talented people and they with you. Everybody wins.

needs? Does it reflect the stage in life you are at today? What additional resources or people would you ideally like to have access to? How can they help you move forward in your life? What do you need to communicate to them so they understand you value their input and ideas? How can you get your success partner, inner circle and/or smart connections supporting you on a regular basis? And, of course, how can you support them?

Although it took time, the effort that Hillary put into building the right support team made her transition to a new position more rewarding than she had anticipated.

> In hindsight, losing my job was the best thing that ever happened to me. Being thrown abruptly into unemployment opened my eyes to the fact that I needed help to get through a difficult professional change. I realized that "going it alone" was not much fun and made things tougher for me than they had to be. When I opened myself up to creating new and meaningful relationships, not only did I expedite my job search but I discovered I felt less burden, less struggle, less loneliness. I now have a success partner, rely on my inner circle for input and sharing, and I've set up a number of smart connections, which just make my life easier.

How you structure your support team will depend on what works best for you. You might find that forming a success partnership provides the connection you are looking for. Alternatively, your perfect support team could consist of your inner circle and a few select smart connections. A monthly supper group plus memberships in a couple of industry associations might meet your needs. Or perhaps weekly e-mails and telephone calls with business colleagues would be ideal. The most important thing is to establish and make a conscious effort to maintain crucial relationships.

Briefcase Moms Balance Zone

Success partner update form

Use these five questions to keep track of your weekly progress when working with a success partner.
- How was last week?
- What are my goals for this meeting?
- What did I accomplish since our last meeting?
- What are the obstacles or opportunities I am facing?
- What are my goals for next week?

9. Practice

Courage

Aspiring to live a life that truly reflects your secret desires can feel pretty daunting and frightening at times. You need to have courage and draw on your inner sources of strength. By boldly facing fear, you will have the conviction to move ahead in spite of your vulnerability. Have the courage to allow space and time for the intimacy you want. Know what fires you up, what stirs your heart. Be passionate about what you do—and, conversely, recognize what doesn't excite you. Get ready for an inspired life.

Intention 25—*Face Your Fears*

Intention 26—*Keep the Fires Burning*

Intention 27—*Be Fully Engaged*

INTENTION 25—

Face Your Fears

If you have worked through the previous eight practices in this book, you have most likely reached a stage where you are gaining clarity on what you want from life. You probably have a pretty good idea what you need to do to achieve your vision.

But having come this far, you may now find yourself facing something that scares the pants off you. It could be anything—letting go of certain responsibilities or relationships, starting a new business, pursuing your dream to travel to South America, transitioning to a four-day workweek, getting married (for a second time).

As your mother used to say, don't worry. As long as you are wearing clean underwear, everything will be all right. Seriously, it's a lot easier to face what's scaring you if you feel some sense of security. On the journey toward balance, that "safe" feeling comes from knowing the type of fear you are experiencing and finding the tools to master it.

> *Life* shrinks or expands in proportion to one's courage.
>
> —ANAÏS NIN

Fear, in all its forms, makes most of us feel unprotected and insecure. It exposes our vulnerability. We become susceptible to the risk of success or failure, to the thoughts and comments of others, to loneliness or to our own inner critic (I'm sure you haven't forgotten her). Yet feeling frightened can also be enlightening. Becoming aware that fear is playing a role in your life is often a gift. It gives you a chance to assess what is holding you back.

Don't be afraid of fear. Instead, expose your fear to the light and determine whether it is real. Fear definitely evokes real physical responses and emotions, yet ironically the fear itself—

the source of your trepidation—may not be real, it may be imagined or the product of worry. When you identify which fears are getting in your way, you can then take all proper and possible precautions to move safely through them. Understanding your fears will help you minimize them as you aim to live a balanced life.

Real fears protect

Let's look first at "real" fear—that is, fear or concern that's based in reality. This is something you are frightened of, or about, that poses a threat or danger to your physical, emotional, professional or social well-being. There are definitely times when we are scared to try something new for some very good reasons. You may experience real fear when taking, or considering, risks associated with your true passion or life's work. The fear you may experience when expressing your innermost feelings or when placing yourself in a situation where others are judging you or that could be dangerous to your body is definitely authentic. Real fear is nature's warning signal, your intuition's way of telling you that something is dangerous. It is important to pay attention to these messages and protect yourself accordingly.

Understanding her real fears enabled Francine, a mother of twin five-year-old girls, to start the business she had envisaged for years. An accountant by trade but an artist at heart, Francine creates striking raku figurines. One of her strong desires, or what she calls her "secret dreams," was to quit her job, rent her own studio and begin selling her pottery on a larger scale. But when I met her, she was holding back from pursuing that vision. She told me she was afraid of being a small-business owner.

With her accounting background, I knew that Francine was better equipped than most people to take care of the operational side of a business. As she explored her fear more closely, she recognized that what was keeping her from entrepreneurship was not what she had originally thought—not having the ability to run her own business. In fact, her fear was not about managing a small business at all. Her fear—a very real one—was being able to generate enough money selling pottery to make her mortgage payments. Her real fear was about starting a business without any financial reserves. We determined how much of a cushion she would require to keep the business going for one year without having to worry about making a profit. Francine then devised a plan that would allow her to save the funds she needed so she could start her business without feeling fearful.

Imagined fears present false blocks

Imagined fear, the second kind of fear we need to acknowledge, is not a healthy type of fear. While real fear is based solidly in the outside environment, imagined fear exists in our head.

Many imagined fears are outcome based—in other words, the source of the fear is attached to an "imagined" end result. Two of our most common fears, of rejection and failure, are both deeply connected to an imagined result. Imagined fear shows up in statements such as the following: "I'm too old to do something new." "I'm so out of shape I'd never be able to do it." "It will take too long." "It will be too hard." "I won't be any good at it." "People will laugh." "I don't have the right training to make it work." "I probably won't be happy doing it." Most of us could fill a page with other examples.

> *It takes a lot of courage to release the familiar and seemingly secure, to embrace the new. But there is no real security in what is no longer meaningful. There is more security in the adventurous and exciting, and in movement there is life, and hope and growth.*
>
> —ALAN COHEN

If you spend all your time fearing an unknown outcome, you may never take a risk. You may never know if you could have competed in that triathlon, given that speech, had that conversation. The secret to releasing imagined fear is to stop worrying about a future you cannot predict. If you move your focus away from a perceived negative result—an unfinished race, an embarrassing public appearance, a lost friend—you allow yourself the opportunity to enjoy the experience of going after what you want. When you detach from the outcome (advice you may remember from the discussion in Intention 7 about finding joy in the doing and not the result), you give yourself the freedom to take chances.

In her early forties, Joan, a buyer for a large department store and mother of a toddler, wanted to take a sabbatical. She had worked for many years without a break, she was tired and feeling uninspired, and she wanted to spend more time with her young daughter. But she was fearful of taking time out. "I am afraid that people will think that I'm a quitter or that I'm unstable. I'm afraid they'll think that I can't handle my job and be a mother at the same time." When Joan faced this fear, she realized that being afraid of what people might think was less persuasive than the good she thought would

Check Your Balance

Carefully assess one of your fears. Is it real, imagined or destructive worry? You can begin this process by writing for ten minutes (one to three pages) in your journal. Try not to edit as you write. Let the thoughts come quickly and easily to the page.

Think about a fear that's been your companion for a while. As you write, from the intuitive side of your brain, the fear that you are assessing will become clearer and clearer. Let your mind leap from one thought about your fear to another. Because fear is often irrational, don't expect your writing about it to be orderly. The point of this exercise is to express your fear, then analyze it. Only when you have determined the type of fear that is holding you back can you begin to deal with it.

come from the downtime. She took her sabbatical. Much to her delight, many of her friends and even some of her colleagues congratulated her and confided that they, too, were considering taking a break from the routine of work.

Change, when it comes, cracks everything open.
—DOROTHY ALLISON

Worry depletes your energy

I used to worry a lot. I worried about money—not having enough or having too much. I worried about what clothes to wear to what event. I worried about whether Adam was going to have friends in school (when he wasn't even out of diapers). I used to waste a lot of time and energy in worry.

Not any more. I still occasionally fret and get what-ifs running through my mind. (I don't know any sane working mother who doesn't.) But I don't let worry dominate my thoughts and freeze me in my tracks.

Learning new patterns to overcome my worry habit made all the difference. I want to share them with you. When I find myself beginning to get anxious, I pay attention to the physical

At the end of three pages, return to the first page and revisit the fear. As you reread what you have written, the fear that you were assessing should seem less of an obstacle. Sometimes just putting something into words pins it down and depletes its ability to hold you back.

For the next month, commit to dropping or ignoring most of your negative, fearful thoughts and worry. Acknowledge these thoughts and emotions for what they are, learn from them, then gently but firmly push them away. As they return, push them away again. You will find that life is a lot more fun without them.

symptoms that accompany that reaction. Is my jaw tightening? Am I furrowing my brow or biting the right side of my lower lip? Can I feel a headache coming on? Am I losing my appetite, a sure sign I'm heading into a fret-fest? Is my sleep interrupted? These are warning signals that I am letting worry take hold.

To redirect myself, I immediately switch my thinking to the now. I focus on what I am doing at the moment—writing, going for a walk, cuddling with Adam. I try to be fully present for at least sixty seconds, then I shift my thoughts to something positive or comforting. By mentally changing gears I stop my mind from going to the what-ifs. This technique has improved my outlook immensely. I am not saying changing gears like this is easy to do, but over time, as I've grown more aware of the signals my body is giving me, I've been able to worry less and be more productive.

As you learn to understand your fears, use your newly unearthed knowledge to your advantage. Let real fear guide you safely to your destination by paying attention to its messages. Analyze your imagined fear and be open to taking some risks. And finally, pledge to not let worry rule your life.

Briefcase Moms Balance Zone
Overcoming fear with four words

Overcoming fear is one of the most challenging tasks you will face on this expedition. Often it's a challenge that's easier faced with company. Let the four T's support you along the way.

Talk—to share with others so fear cannot be your only companion.
Truth—to expose fear for what it is.
Trust—to guide you along the right path you are taking.
Time— to let you enjoy the process.

INTENTION 26 —

Keep the Fires Burning

The toys are put away, the homework is done and the kids are in bed. The lunches are made and the dishwasher is on. You wash your face, brush your teeth, choose clothes for tomorrow and then collapse into bed beside your spouse. You lean over to give your mate a perfunctory kiss and casually comment that your sex life "sure isn't what it used to be before kids"—and instantly fall asleep.

It's a familiar scenario that finds its way into jokes and television sitcoms. Nurturing love, intimacy and romance can often drop to the bottom of the list for working parents. And it is easy to understand how this happens. Leaving your love life to the last may not be intentional—it may just be the result of a jam-packed existence. In a working parent's world there is always some commitment or task that you or your partner feel you must attend to before taking time for your intimate relationship.

> *One touch is worth ten thousand words.*
>
> —HAROLD BLOOMFIELD

I've heard it said that modern-day couples are so overwhelmed with the daily grind that sex-absent marriages in North America are reaching epidemic proportions. Sleep has become what people crave, not sex. Though I'm all in favor of a good night's sleep (see Intention 8), if you get in the habit of forfeiting time for intimacy for some extra shut-eye, you can easily compromise the balance in your relationship.

Remember when you first met? You could hardly wait to see each other. Every look, every touch was electric. You loved being with one another. And romance was everywhere, from candlelit dinners to uninterrupted intimate conversations. What happened? Where did all that wonderful stuff you experienced with your soul mate go?

Well, becoming parents is definitely a desire-buster. The responsibility of caring for an infant, sleep deprivation and juggling the roles of parent and lover can take their toll on intimacy. The intensity of new parenthood eventually wanes; however, many couples unfortunately establish behavior patterns at this time that last for years. The most debilitating pattern is one that takes your romantic relationship for granted or lets your bond with your child overshadow your connection with one other.

To keep the fires burning in your relationship calls for courage. Though this may, at first, seem an odd statement, it is true. By becoming parents, you have risked your love life by introducing new people into the family mix. It is easier to revel in the unquestioning need your children have for you than to risk re-establishing your relationship with your partner on new terms. Regenerating passion, deepening intimacy and growing together in the ever-changing dynamic of working parenthood is not necessarily easy, but, with courage and commitment, it can be done.

Check Your Balance

To get your intimate life back on track, you must know what you want. Consider the following questions, then choose three that resonate with you to write about. Take some time with your journal to write whatever comes into your mind as you consider these questions. Write without pausing to criticize your writing or edit yourself.

- What does romance mean to me?
- What does intimacy mean to me? Is it the same or different than romance?
- What do I want in my love life?
- What is the perfect romantic gesture?
- What does an ideal romantic date look like?
- How intimately connected am I with my partner right now?
- What does great sex mean to me?

Communicate lovingly

Speak your truth...tactfully. The foundation of a satisfying intimate relationship is in knowing and understanding each other's desires and dreams. For this reason, make an effort to share your romantic needs and sexual wants, rather than keeping them a secret. If you are the more highly sexed spouse, explain your feelings to your partner. If a little more help around the house will make you feel more amorous, tell your mate. If you don't know what your lover wants/likes and vice versa, you both could be heading into trouble. Keeping quiet or getting upset and resentful are not very good aphrodisiacs.

Often we may think we know what the other person is thinking or feeling, but if you have not checked in with your mate lately, you could be on the wrong track. And if your partner doesn't know that you need a little romance time, you can't expect to get it. Better to speak about it honestly and lovingly, even though you may feel like you're exposing yourself to rejection, than to harbor anger. (To handle the imagined fear of rejection, revisit Intention 25.)

- Do my partner and I have evenly matched libidos?
- How can I increase intimacy in my relationship?
- How do I communicate my romantic needs and sexual wants to my partner?

To create, maintain and enhance passion in your relationship with your mate takes courage. Feeling nervous about making changes in the romance department can be interpreted as excitement, which means you are ready to play a bigger and better game with your lover.

Create space for intimacy

Make space in your schedule for intimacy. I know this does not sound very romantic or spontaneous. But if you are like most North American working women, if you don't "pencil in" some romance time, you might find it just doesn't happen. You'll find that when a "date night" is in your calendar, you start to look forward to it and that can become a turn-on. And scheduling time to connect with your partner at a deeper level than "What's for dinner?" and "Who's picking up the kids?" will strengthen your bond.

Accustom *yourself continually to make many acts of love, for they enkindle and melt the soul.*

—SAINT TERESA OF AVILA

Save space in your mind for sexy and romantic thoughts. See what happens when you take some time just to "think" about sex. Studies have shown that women who read romance novels make love more often. Designate a special place or activity as your romantic kick-starter. This could be a favorite walk, restaurant or room in your home. Know you and your mate could go to this location and the feeling of romance would instantly be in the air. Ensure that you can relax in the place where you make love most often (for North Americans it's the bedroom) and set the stage for uninterrupted pleasure. With kids in the house, this may mean getting a lock for your bedroom door so that you can enjoy yourself without worrying about unexpected visits.

Remember time for you

Before there is "us" time, there needs to be "you" time. In other words, take an interest in your personal needs and give yourself permission to take care of yourself first, as discussed in Intention 1. This is an essential prerequisite for an intimate and giving relationship with someone else. When you are feeling valued, relaxed, healthy and worry-free, you will have more of yourself to share with someone special.

Briefcase Moms Balance Zone

Intimacy-starters

Light some candles for instant atmosphere.

Take a bath. Better yet, take a candlelit bath.

Open a bottle of champagne. Champagne for no reason will make your partner feel very special.

Write a love note. Surprise your lover with a card or letter, perhaps left in the sock drawer.

Hire a babysitter. Time alone together is a must.

Talk. Listen.

Intimacy-killers

Television.	To turn your partner on, you must turn the TV set off.
Criticism.	Encourage one another to experience total acceptance in and out of the bedroom.
Stress.	An irritated mind douses the flames of passion.
No sleep.	Not enough sleep really does mean you are too tired.
Too busy.	If you are always working, there is no time for love.
Preoccupation.	Leave your work thoughts at the office.

INTENTION 27—

Be Fully Engaged

Heather, a forty-year-old mother of two school-age daughters, like many other working mothers I know, was desperately seeking a career that meant something to her. Here's how she explained her situation to me.

> I am not quite sure how I have arrived at this crossroads in my life. Why did I become a hospital administrator? I have absolutely no passion for this position. My job is incredibly boring for me, but I have it really good here. I am compensated well and have great health benefits. It's a good organization to work for and it allows me the flexibility I'm looking for as a working mom. But I'm not challenged. I want to be as excited about my work as I am about other areas of my life.

Many women are looking for personal satisfaction in professional accomplishment. We want to thrive in a workplace that allows us to express our true selves and honor our values. For some, a vocation that fosters our creativity, challenges our mind and stimulates our soul is essential.

Having said all that, most working moms also want a life—a life that includes work but is not completely dominated by it. You want to be fully engaged in, to feel passionate about, all aspects of your life.

You cannot be really first-rate at your work if your work is all you are. —ANNA QUINDLEN

Being fully engaged can take many forms and will look different for each woman reading this book. You can find your passion in your work, your family, your volunteerism, your hobby and more. It is not something that appears or arrives from nowhere. Passion is the result or by-product of doing something that excites you to your core. It comes from taking action and being involved in something that truly holds your attention. Your passion may reside in one area, like work, but most likely will be found in a combination of arenas. No matter what your particular definition of living passionately, the results are the same for all—feeling connected with yourself and others, energized and joyous.

I have seen that a key to a working mom's ability to live a fully engaged life is determining the role of her career in her life. Put another way, how do your competing passions of career, family and volunteerism, to name a few, fit together? Like so many aspects of balance in our lives, the ideal career engagement each of us requires to achieve fulfillment is unique. It can range from simply feeling happier on the job to accepting nothing less than being completely passionate and inspired. Our individual needs and circumstances will dictate why (and whether) we are seeking more from our careers than a paycheck. We needn't feel badly for being at either end of the spectrum, as long as we have made a conscious choice—and are clear about how the pieces of the puzzle interlock to create the passion-filled picture we really want.

For the most part, Americans rate satisfaction with their personal lives highly: 78% score their satisfaction at 4 or 5 on a 5-point scale. But engaged workers are much more likely to respond with 5s (65%) than 4s (27%). "Not-engaged" workers (those who aren't engaged with their work but aren't actively disenchanted) are less likely to respond with 5s (36%) than 4s (42%).

—Gallup's Employee Engagement Index,
interviews conducted October 2000–March 2003

It could be that being engaged in your career means you work for an organization that you truly believe in, but the job you hold does not inspire you. Say, for example, you're the purchasing manager—something you're not wild about—for a pediatric cancer clinic, an organization that truly speaks to your soul. It's being involved with the organization, not necessarily doing your job, that raises your enthusiasm.

Alternatively, you may crave a career that you care deeply about, that is motivating and meaningful. Here it is the job itself—the day-to-day work you do personally—that must enthuse you. Career engagement might also mean that you find your passions outside your work. (I know that sounds counterintuitive, but think categories of engagement.) It might be that your work is still important to you, but you find fulfillment through personal interests such as mountain biking, teaching new immigrants to read or writing poetry.

Be really whole and all things will come to you.
—LAO-TZU

For Heather, understanding the role she wanted her career to play in her life would provide her with guidelines to

Check Your Balance

Determining your ideal career engagement is integral to feeling passionate about your life. If professional accomplishment and a values match will ensure you feel fulfilled at work, and you've achieved that, you will feel a sense of balance and the freedom to commit elsewhere. However, if your desired level of engagement is out of sync with your day-to-day professional life, a sense of unbalance and dissatis-

faction may result. To better understand what will enable you to be fully passionate about the life you're choosing, open your journal and answer the following questions:

- What do I feel is the purpose of my work?
- How does my work life fit into my larger life?
- Am I passionate about the work I do? Is that important?
- Do I experience passion outside my work?
- What originally attracted me to

move forward. I asked her to consider four categories of career engagement: professional accomplishment, values match, purpose and passion. One of these would best meet her need to feel fulfilled.

> In reviewing the categories of career engagement I figured out that I had both a sense of accomplishment and a values match at work, yet I wanted more...but not as much as I had originally thought. I realized that I was okay with not being "passionate" about my job every day. I experience passion in many other areas of my life. But what I did want was to feel more of a sense of purpose at work.
>
> When I looked back at what had originally engaged me in my work, it was helping people. I started out as a nurse and I loved that connection with patients and the sense of contribution that caring for others allowed me. As I've advanced in my career I've moved further and further away from what was originally important to me. I know that for me to enjoy work again I must find a way to have contact with patients. I'm not sure yet how that will come about, but I feel much better having identified what was "missing."

Like Heather, when you look at your level of career engagement, you will gain a new perspective on your work and life.

the career path I have followed?

- What originally attracted me to the job I have now?
- What do I like about my work?
- What is it about my current job that I dislike? What is missing?
- Am I feeling bored at work? If so, can I identify one or two of the sources of my boredom?
- Do my core values match those of the organization I work with?
- When was the last time I was fully absorbed at work?

Next, review the four career engagement categories and decide where you are in each. Also think about where you want to be. Once you've determined the kind of engagement that will bring you fulfillment at work, try to identify three changes you can make to bring you closer to operating at your ideal level. This could mean scaling down your involvement or notching it up. Tap into your inner courage and commit to making a change in either direction.

Levels of career engagement

Professional accomplishment
Doing work that is interesting to you and enables you to feel as if you are reaching your professional goals results in a professional accomplishment. For example, meeting quota if you are in sales or providing effective estate planning if you are a tax specialist.

Values match
When you are performing work that supports your personal core values (see Intention 13), a values match results. Are your values aligned with the values of the organization you work with or own? The closer your values are to the organization's, the greater your work satisfaction and happiness are likely to be. To get a values match, you must clearly understand not only your own core values, but also the culture and values of any organization you wish to work for or with.

Purpose
To have purpose is to do something you truly believe in— small or big. It could be making a contribution to something larger than yourself. Purpose is connected with making a difference, whether at a family, community, national or global level. If you are finding purpose in your career, most likely you are also meeting your professional goals and the values of the organization match your own. But purpose should not be confused with passion.

Passion
If you are engaged in your work at a high level, emotionally and technically, passion follows. When passion is present, you are often fully absorbed, and hours slip away from you unnoticed. This is called being "in the flow"—you are continually focused and inspired.

10. Practice

Reflection

When you are near the end of a journey, it is very satisfying to trace where you have been on the map, leaf through your travel diary and review your photos. Now it's time to reflect on the expedition you've undertaken to travel your own personal route to balanced living. It's time to notice and celebrate your accomplishments. Look how far you've come. Look how your attitudes have changed. Acknowledge your insights and what you have learned. Reward your efforts. Most importantly, ask the question, where do I go from here?

Intention 28—*Craft a Life Theme*

Intention 29—*Let the Light Shine*

Intention 30—*Redefine Having It All*

INTENTION 28—

Craft a Life Theme

As you move into the final three intentions of this book, now is a great time to reflect on all you've learned and done to create a more balanced life. Maybe you've defined a dream. Perhaps obstacles have been exposed and blown to bits. You might have developed a balance vision and new attitudes, and are striding ahead in your life with more direction and purpose than ever before. Whatever life transformation has taken place—whether a new thought, approach or relationship—it is worthy of celebration.

We intuitively know how important it is to acknowledge and reward accomplishment. We do it for others all the time. We praise friends, congratulate colleagues or staff on a job well done, and encourage our spouse and children. Yet when it comes to giving ourselves a pat on the back, to honoring our successes, we're not so at ease. I've noticed that working mothers often immediately move on to the next thing on the to-do list after finishing a project or reaching a goal, without pausing to contemplate their achievements.

Celebrate you

By constantly pushing forward to the next thing, without adequate respect for and recognition of what you've achieved, you can diminish the value of your wins in your own mind and the minds of others. If you never take the time to think about and appreciate your accomplishments and reward yourself accordingly, it is as if your successes have never happened. If you've ever been in a work situation where your team leader never bothered to acknowledge or congratulate your hard work, but instead simply loaded on the next task, you will know what this feels like from the inside. It can be demoralizing. So if you find yourself making light of your successes or, worse, not mentioning them at all, it's time to change that pattern of behavior.

Celebrate what you want to see more of.

—TOM PETERS

Start with making a conscious effort to congratulate and reward yourself. There are many ways, large and small, to recognize and honor your accomplishments. While writing this book I set up a personal reward system. As I mentioned before, it's a challenge for me to sit for extended periods of time at my computer writing without any interaction with other human beings. My reward for staying focused and keeping my fingers to the keyboard during the mornings was to call a friend in the afternoons. Connecting with people close to me was my prize. My rewards for reaching major milestones in the writing process were more substantial and tended to expand my wardrobe. When I finished writing the first twenty intentions, I bought myself a stunning pair of blue and cream suede shoes that I'd been coveting for weeks. (Wouldn't any normal, shoe-loving fanatic?) Consider how you want to celebrate the changes you've made and the insights you've achieved as you've worked through this book.

I celebrate myself, and sing myself.

—WALT WHITMAN

Create your life theme

At the start of each year I ask my clients to forget making New Year's resolutions. I don't believe in them. I don't think they work because they are often based on "shoulds" versus the bigger picture of a person's life. How many people do you know who, in January, enthusiastically name their resolution for the year yet somehow neglect to follow through with it a few weeks or months later? Like I said, they rarely work. What I've found does work is creating a life theme for the year ahead.

As you read the final pages in this book, it is like coming to a year-end of sorts. All that you have discovered about yourself—what's important to you, the areas of your life you want to change—is setting the stage for the next phase of your life. It's a beginning for you and a very appropriate time to create your life theme. (If you happen to be reading this passage in the month of December, you've got the syn-chronicity of the calendar year, too.) Your life theme will be your overriding intention or "big picture" focus for the up-coming months. It has an expiration date of December 31, when you'll get a chance to re-evaluate your direction.

Having a life theme is like having a personal mission state-

Check Your Balance

It's time to brag and boast a little. Open your journal to a place where two blank pages face each other. Title the left-hand page "Accom-plishments." Title the right-hand page "Rewards." To support you in identifying all you have achieved so far toward living a balanced life, review the following questions as you leaf through the written pages of your journal.

- What new thoughts, insights or ideas have I had?
- What changes (small or large) have I made to bring more balance into my life?
- How have I grown as a person, a mother, a professional?
- In general, what have I accom-plished in my life so far for my family and my career and me?
- What am I most proud of?

Now fill that left-hand page by listing every accomplishment you

ment for your whole life, personal and professional, updated annually. A life theme works because it takes into consideration and connects all your intentions for the year in a succinct and powerful phrase. This collection of one to five words describes what you want to accomplish in all areas of your life and cements your main priorities with intended action.

As you've written in your journal and worked through the exercises in this book, perhaps you've come back to "well-being" or "wellness" over and over. Maybe the theme "improving relationships" has impacted you the most. It could be that what's tugged at your heart repeatedly is "being passionate." Or perhaps you've focused on "lightening up." All these are clues to support you in crafting your life theme based on what you think will bring you balance and what you want to achieve both personally and professionally.

Maybe you've recognized that you haven't made time in your life for many friends, that your networks are weak and that you'd like to have a social circle beyond your immediate family. To turn this around, your life theme could be "Connection." Perhaps you've realized that your life is far more filled with work and errands than with fun and play, and you want to fix that imbalance. "Energize" could be a life

can think of, from a simple insight to a major behavioral change, that has resulted from reading this book and doing the exercises in it. Write one item on each line. When you've filled the page (and this list need not be exhaustive, by any means), turn your attention to the facing page. For each accomplishment on the left-hand page, list a corresponding reward on the right-hand page. The rewards could be big or small: "Drink my favorite latte." "Take

myself to the beach for an hour." "On Saturday afternoon, read that novel I've wanted to." "Book a facial." Beside each reward, indicate a date by which you will reap the reward. This is a must-do step. And when you reap the reward, remember what you have accomplished. You are celebrating you.

Next, meditate or concentrate on developing your life theme. Commit the next five minutes to thoughtful analysis. You don't have to write

continued on next page

theme that changes the situation.

My life theme during the months and months I spent writing this book was "Completion." I loved this word—it sang to me and I knew exactly what it meant in the context of my personal challenges and choices. When I came up with the theme "Completion," not only did I have a book I wanted to finish writing, I had a number of home renovation projects I wanted to complete, too (was I crazy?). I used my theme as a filter for all my decisions about how I spent my time, money and energy. I only said yes to those things that fit within my overall intention of completion. What I noticed was that focusing on this intention gave me great direction and things fell into place as a result. (You're reading one end product, and the important home projects got done, too.) Your theme needs to strike an emotional chord with you and bring a smile to your face when you say it. You must own it. You must feel your theme's magic. It must propel you forward.

You cannot change your destination overnight, but you can change your direction.

—Jim Rohn

anything down at this point. Just ask your wise self what your theme is—she knows. She may not tell you right away, but by making the request now, the right phrase will come to you. If it doesn't arrive immediately, don't worry. It will. Just having the intention to discover your life theme will support you in making it happen.

When the phrase does reveal itself to you, try to keep it to a maximum of five words. Brief is better.

Feel the power of these concise life themes: Let Go. Rebuild. Move Forward. Growth and Independence. Balance and Follow-Through. Connection. Some of you will recognize your life theme right away; others might have to live with it for a week or so before knowing it's the one that will speak to you for the next year. You will know when you've got it.

Once your life theme is clear, write it down. Put it where you will see it every day.

Briefcase Moms Balance Zone

Life themes

Below is a brief list of some of the life themes my clients have created.

Coming Together	Dialing Back
Abundance	Authentic Passion
Creating Community	Moderation
Fun and Laughter	Collaboration
Simplicity	Stretch
Transition and Creativity	Calm and Quiet

INTENTION 29—

Let the Light Shine

We are all creative beings with unique talents and experiences that cause us to participate in and view the world through a distinctive, highly customized lens. As you've navigated your way through this book, I imagine that some parts of it have resonated with you more strongly than others. What has sparked emotion or captivated you will depend on your own personal perspective—who you are as an individual, your life circumstances and your belief systems.

Some intentions will have motivated you more than others. Some Check Your Balance exercises you will have readily chosen to ponder and work on, writing easily in your journal as thoughts and feelings flowed from your pen. Which intentions and exercises you've willingly and eagerly worked on will tell you as much about yourself as the ones you found difficult. If you are particularly resistant to a concept, philosophy or strategy, ask yourself what's getting in your way. Often what we avoid can be the source of our biggest blocks, and you know my thoughts on obstacles...KABOOM!

The same can be said about how you continue toward balanced living. Your success will depend greatly on the attitude you choose to adopt. You can consciously choose to adjust the lens through which you experience the world. You can choose to let in more light or shut it out. When you trust yourself, focus on gratitude and believe in abundance, you will experience more light. You will shine from within. Life will feel easier, more peaceful. You will be more carefree, more content. Your strongest ally in finding balance will be your belief in yourself.

Let your light shine. Shine within you so that it can shine on someone else. Let your light shine.
—OPRAH WINFREY

Trust yourself enough to grow

Trust is such a loaded word. Many mothers juggling family and work would define trust as believing in, having faith in or being dependent on someone else. And that can be comfortable

---

Check Your Balance

You are what you focus on. Take the next fifteen minutes to explore your thoughts regarding trust, gratitude and abundance. To do this, find a quiet spot in which to sit and think about whether you agree or disagree with the following statements. Your response will tell you a lot about your attitudes.

- I have a strong sense of self and trust my intuition, instincts and inner direction.
- I rely on outside opinions to make big decisions in my life.
- I take the time to regularly check in with my inner wisdom.
- I believe I know what is best for me.
- I often compare myself to others.
- I base my self-worth on how I measure up compared to my colleagues and friends.
- I don't think I will ever have enough to be truly satisfied.
- I believe in abundance but there never seems to be enough for me.

or uncomfortable, depending on our life experiences up till now. However, what if you take the "someone else" out of the equation and concentrate on you, on trusting in yourself? Without this personal trust, you will struggle more than you need to.

Karli, a single mom of two school-age boys, was finding it difficult to achieve the move from teacher to vice-principal, a job change she really wanted. She had done her research and several interviews but had not yet been successful. Compared to other women she knew, Karli felt her life was a mess. In her eyes, these women had great jobs, perfect kids (remember, no such thing is possible), stylish clothes, exciting careers, a wonderful home and considerate partners. She, on the other hand, had a messy house, credit card debt, a job she couldn't seem to move beyond, lovely but very demanding children and a communication problem with her ex-husband.

It was clear that Karli didn't trust in herself. Somewhere over the years, she had lost that inner trust she had taken for granted in her early twenties. Now she looked outside for confirmation that she was okay. And she couldn't find that validation by comparing herself and her situation, which she knew so well, to other women she saw and the lives they

- I know the universe will provide for my every need.
- I understand the law of abundance and have experienced it in my life.
- I regularly take an inventory of my life's assets: family, friends, home and health.
- I practice gratitude on a daily basis.

If your responses to these statements lead you to want to shift your attitudes, use your journal to help you get there. Begin by practicing gratitude on a daily basis. For the next week, list in your journal five things you are thankful for each day. On challenging days you may only be able to list the basics, like "I'm still breathing." On other days you may be able to articulate some very joyful moments and gifts.

continued on next page

presented to the outside world. For, of course, it was an unfair comparison. Karli felt she didn't measure up to some ideal, imaginary standard. She was filled with envy, resentment and anger about what seemed to be missing from her life, but seemed evident in others' lives. Much to her chagrin, she found herself saying to her children, "Why can't you be good like Brooke and Michael next door?" She wanted to release this destructive practice of comparison. To make that happen, I encouraged her to believe in herself again and recognize the gifts that were already present in her life. Having faith in her abilities to live the life she desired was a first step in creating the frame of mind that would lead her to success. But it was just the beginning.

Focus on gratitude and abundance

Each of us has many things to be grateful for in our lives. But sometimes we take them for granted or, even worse, we forget them in the midst of our crowded daily schedules. Like Karli, we can sometimes focus on what we don't have instead of treasuring what we do.

One of my clients adopted a personal abundance statement that she could turn to when she was feeling overwhelmed. It read: "There is enough. There will be enough. I am enough." Simple. Powerful. If you are ready to take things a step further, write your own abundance statement of twenty words or less. What does abundance mean to you?

Life is not always perfect (it's not supposed to be) nor does it always go our way, but focusing on the negative drags us down and depletes the energy we need to advance. Instead, when you acknowledge what is working, when you are grateful for the simple joys of life (see Intention 7), like a hug from your child, you become more aware of the goodness that surrounds you each day. Awareness of that goodness will invigorate you and support you in overcoming difficulties. This practice of daily gratitude slows life down and makes it much more joyful.

Gratitude unlocks the fullness of life. It turns what we have into enough, and more. It turns denial into acceptance, chaos to order, confusion to clarity. It can turn a meal into a feast, a house into a home, a stranger into a friend. Gratitude makes sense of our past, brings peace for today, and creates a vision for tomorrow.

—MELODY BEATTIE

To shift from an attitude of scarcity (focusing on what was missing for her) to one of abundance (knowing there was enough for all), Karli agreed to acknowledge all the positives in her life each day. Instead of concentrating on her messy house, she was grateful that she had a safe and comfortable home. She made an effort to be really aware during her precious moments with her children rather than obsessing about the times they were exuberant and wild. The more attention Karli paid to the blessings in her life, the happier and more fulfilled she became.

After a few months of concentrating on trusting herself and acknowledging what she was grateful for, Karli began to notice that her attitude was shifting toward abundance without her making a conscious effort. Now that she appreciated what she had in her life, she no longer made those demoralizing comparisons. Karli still held onto her dream of becoming a vice-principal and continued to work toward it, but she no longer felt angry that she hadn't yet made that career leap. Through the practice of gratitude she had rediscovered the pleasure she felt in helping students learn. The lens through which Karli viewed the world was now letting in more light.

Expect your every need to be met,
Expect the answer to every problem,
Expect abundance on every level,
Expect to grow spiritually.

—EILEEN CADDY

Briefcase Moms Balance Zone
Stop comparing. Start empathizing. Keep supporting.

Women have a tendency to compare their insides (what's really going on in their lives) with other women's outsides (what they present to the outer world). This is like comparing apples to bananas and often results in unrealistic expectations, envy and resentment. Instead, if you take an empathetic look at your situation and those of the women around you, internal validation will start to displace external comparisons. When this happens, you will be better able to emotionally support yourself and other women. Instead of comparing and downgrading yourself, leverage the value of women empowering women.

INTENTION 30—
Redefine Having It All

Because of the work I do, I pay particular attention to studies, magazine and newspaper articles, and conversations that explore working mothers' challenges and successes. One recent article sparked my ire. I was disturbed not so much by the content of the piece as by the conclusion. The writer summed up by saying it was clear that working mothers could not have it all. We could "have our cake, but we definitely couldn't eat it." This statement, you know if you read the introduction to this book, I wholeheartedly disagree with.

Through my personal experiences, my clients' wisdom and the conversations I have had with women combining careers and motherhood, I have been privileged to see first-hand that working mothers are redefining what "having it all" means to them and rediscovering balance on their own terms. I have shared my and other women's stories in these pages to illustrate that you can find harmony in all the areas of your life—your career, your family and your own personal satisfaction—when you make conscious choices that bring you joy and fulfillment. What I hope has been clearly conveyed is that the secret to having and eating your cake is knowing what kind of cake you want—carrot, angel food, cheesecake, pineapple upside-down cake. Women who balance raising children, finding joy in their careers and pursing their own dreams choose cakes containing the ingredients they love and savor every bite. They live their lives based on their priorities and passions…and they define balance in their own way.

In this book I have attempted to pass on practices that make it easier for you to balance your life. Our conversation has not been so much about "how to do everything." Rather, I hope you've contemplated who you want to be and what you want to do in order to have what you want. I am passionate about this approach to life because when you truly understand who you are, what you want and how you wish to obtain it, life becomes intensely satisfying and rewarding.

First choose who you want to be

Many of us have been conditioned to spend our lives doing things—getting the right education, finding the perfect job, making sacrifices to get ahead—to enable us to acquire the material things we want, whether a big house, a fancy car or a country club membership, so we will be happy, fulfilled and successful. However, plenty of tense, unhappy and stressed women among us, despite having many things, including the accessories of success, still feel that something is missing. In my view, they definitely don't have it all.

Often people attempt to live their lives backwards: they try to have more things, or more money, in order to do more of what they want so that they will be happier. The way it actually works is the reverse. You must first be who you really are, then, do what you need to do, in order to have what you want.

—Margaret Young

Truly having it all results when you change this traditional order. Rather than focusing on what you *want* to have, first choose *who* you want to be and become (see Intention 11 again for more details). If being happy, fulfilled and engaged are characteristics of the person you are striving to become, then do the things you need to do to create that transformation. When you are who you want to be, you will end up having everything you want.

This means making sure that what you want out of life is

congruent with the person you are. It means the career you choose, the life decisions you make, must line up with your goals and priorities. When these three areas of your life are aligned, you will experience much less pain, sacrifice and envy. These emotions will be replaced by a sense of peace—a feeling that you are doing the right thing (for you and your family) and that everything is falling into place. There may still be hard work involved, but you will encounter far less resentment and struggle. You will still have to determine the right ingredients for your cake, but you can choose who bakes it—you, your sister, your neighborhood bakery. By making choices that align who you are, what you want and how you get it, you *can* have your cake and eat it, too.

If you know you are a quiet, introspective person and you want a moderate work schedule that allows time for you also to express yourself creatively, then having and eating your cake means steering clear of a career goal to be CEO of a Fortune 500 company. No matter how inviting that may look from the outside, it won't define success for you. However, the opposite will be true if you enjoy leading others and thrive in a climate of professional growth and responsibility. If you know you are a person who craves adventure, loves travel and really enjoys connecting with new people, then reconsider that purchase of a large house in the suburbs that leaves you stretched financially and limits your ability to see new places. That may be someone *else's* dream for you, but it is not yours. If you recognize that making a contribution and motivating others is your passion, then choosing to be a teacher or a mentor in your profession aligns who you are, what you want and how you get it. Your options are limitless, as long as they are the right fit for you.

Understand what you want

When you understand your true self, know what you want

and choose your path wisely, you open yourself up for a life that is fulfilling and happy no matter what you tackle. Of course, this may mean making some tough choices and not-so-easy decisions, but the lifetime results will be worth it. Such was the case for Nicole.

A partner in a multinational management-consulting firm, with two school-age children and a spouse in an equally demanding job, Nicole was feeling harried and hurried. She decided after much reflection that she didn't want to continue having stress in the family, being away on trips, managing the nanny and having little time for personal relationships. She recently resigned and is now in the process of redefining what she wants to do, which she believes will be something that better aligns with her values and balance vision (see Intention 22). Right now she is leaning toward something more flexible, more entrepreneurial. This was not a simple decision for Nicole to make, but as a team with her partner, she made this choice.

Another client, Sheila, decided to make some significant changes, too, but they turned out to be completely different from what she originally thought was needed to balance her life. Holding a senior position in a national insurance company, raising three school-age children and juggling several volunteer positions left Sheila contemplating a new career. After three months of intensive coaching, Sheila came to realize that she did not want to leave her career. In fact, she treasured the respect, recognition and knowledge she had gained from her twenty years of experience and very much enjoyed the environment she worked in. Sheila discovered that reorganizing the way she worked, taking time for her self-care and reassessing some volunteer work made all the difference. She didn't want to quit her job. She wanted to do more of what she loved professionally. Sheila let go of what was no longer serving her. She is still fine-tuning but fundamentally she is very satisfied with her choices.

Choose your path intentionally

I suspect that you, like Nicole and Sheila, have come to know yourself better through the active self-analysis, contemplation and writing you have done with the help of this book. You have probably found it easier to identify your real wants and priorities.

As you've considered and written, thought and acted while reading this book, you will have discovered that in some areas of your life you are further along the road to balance than you might have thought before you began. I hope, too, that you have been reminded of the richness and wonder of your life. I would like to think you've flagged the pages of this book you've found helpful and highlighted the passages you wish to refer to often. I hope you've filled your journal with insights and confirmations and experienced the value in writing down your heart's desire.

The self-knowledge you have gained by working through this book will set the direction for your life. The route you choose to take can be one of ease and grace—or struggle and effort. That is the choice you have to make now as you close this book.

You can have it all on your terms. You have all the wisdom, all the power to start living the life you want right now—a life that combines your passion for your children, your career and your own fulfillment.

Choose your cake and eat it, too. All the right ingredients are within your reach. Savor your life. Share it with family and friends. Enjoy every mouthful.

According to Hindu legend, long ago all humans were gods. But they so abused the privilege that Brahma, the god of all gods, decided their wisdom and power should be taken away from them. But he had to hide it where no human would ever find it again.

"Let us bury it deep within the earth," suggested one god. Brahma said, "No, they will dig until they find it."

"Let us throw it into the deepest part of the biggest ocean," proposed another god.

"Humans will learn to dive and someday come across it," insisted Brahma.

"Then it can be hidden in the clouds atop the highest mountain of the Himalayas."

"They will manage to climb that high someday," Brahma pointed out. "I have a better idea. Let us hide it where they will never think to look: inside themselves."

Check Your Balance

Now is the time to pause and reflect. Where do you go from here? Take some time to read through your journal entries and be a student of your own life. As you look back through the record of the journey you've taken with this book, ask what is the most valuable discovery you've made about yourself. Pay attention to those ideas, inklings and insights you've put to paper. Pull out your key findings and collect them in a summary sheet at the back of your journal.

Give yourself permission and the space to start intentionally changing your life by making a plan to take action on those things you've identified that will bring you the greatest joy.

A Vision and Epilogue

Happy, Healthy, Balanced Children

By now you know I am passionate about helping women live balanced lives while raising children, finding joy in their careers and fulfilling their dreams. It's been my good fortune to see that mothers who are committed to finding a balance (individually discovered and defined) of work, family and personal pursuits live happily and passionately. They are wonderful role models for their children.

Our children learn mainly from who we are, not what we say we are. They follow our actions and not necessarily our words. How you act in the world is one of the greatest influences on your children. They look to you as a model to determine what is appropriate behavior. To see you growing, learning and enjoying life is one of the greatest gifts you can give your children. Enriching your life enriches your child's life.

This overriding belief drives my vision, mission and purpose. It is the foundation and reason for this book and all that is done at Briefcase Moms®, my coaching and personal development company for working mothers.

It is my vision that all children have the opportunity to be happy, healthy and balanced. Therefore, my mission is to make it easier for working mothers to live balanced and successful lives and to inspire their children to do the same. My goal is to create a movement to empower one million career-oriented mothers to find a better balance. I need your help to do that.

I've always believed that one woman's success can only help another woman's success.
—GLORIA VANDERBILT

The Briefcase Moms® Revolution

I hope that by reading this book you are inspired to be a part of the Briefcase Moms® revolution—a community of women, just like you, who are committed to reaching their vision of work and family balance, while creating a life reflecting their values, passions and desires. We need more advocates. We need more women to champion this cause. We need women like you who want to bring more balance into their own lives and help other working mothers reach their balance vision.

We women can, and do, learn so much from each other. By helping other working mothers live balanced lives, you will be making a valuable contribution to our world. If you have gained some insight or learned some new techniques on how to better balance children, career and self, share this with other women you know who struggle with issues of work-life balance. Yours will be a much-treasured gift.

It is extremely fulfilling to make a difference in someone's life. When you help another working mother define and achieve balanced living on her terms, you will gain personally from your generosity. It just feels good to make another woman smile.

> *The* greatest challenge of the day is how to bring about a revolution of the heart, a revolution that has to start with each one of us.
>
> —DOROTHY DAY

There are four ways you can champion the Briefcase Moms® revolution. Do whatever you can, whatever matches your time, energy and resources.

1. *Form your own Briefcase Moms® Circle.* Leverage the knowledge and experience of other women by putting together a group to do the work in this book. Set the parameters for your circle up front, such as the frequency and location of your meetings and the pace for moving through the book. Support and accountability from a group will increase the impact and integration of the book's practices and intentions in your life.

2. *Participate in the Briefcase Moms® Program.* From the comfort of your own home or office, you will connect with other like-minded working mothers and work through the practices and intentions in this book. I lead this virtual seminar series and guarantee it will give you the tools to achieve your own ideal life balance as well as the tools to help you spread the word to others.

3. *Be a workplace change agent.* Aim to communicate the benefits of a family-friendly workplace. Do your part to foster a corporate culture that has positive work-life balance policies and programs, plus flexible scheduling, female advancement and child care options.

4. *Spread the word.* Tell other working mothers about the Briefcase Moms® revolution. Let them know there is something they can do to improve their situation. Encourage them to read this book. You can direct them to my website, www.briefcasemoms.com, and suggest they sign up to receive my on-line newsletter.

Mahatma Gandhi said, "Be the change you want to see in the world." Seize the opportunity to intentionally change your life now—and experience the ripple effect of your efforts. My experience as a life coach tells me that having read this book, the best thing you can do now is take action.

Acknowledgments

As I write these final words I am overflowing with gratitude. I am grateful to be finished writing and birthing this book (it's been a very long labor) and even more thankful for the tremendous support I've been privileged to receive.

This book would not be possible without my clients, who placed their trust and confidence in me to help them bring more balance to their lives. Your personal stories form the backbone of this book. Thank you for inspiring me and sharing your experiences. It's been wonderful learning together.

Many midwives helped this book on its way to life. Without their involvement, it would still be thoughts in my head and a few scribbles in my notebook. My sincere thanks go to:

My editor, Judith Walker, whose guiding hand helped shape and reshape the words on the page. I still remember our first meeting and just knowing you were the perfect editor for this project. And you've been more than that— your faith, talent and grace throughout this process have been an inspiration. You kept me going on many a day when I felt like letting things slide. Thank you for those Friday morning calls.

Carol Rial, who went above and beyond the call of duty, walking several cold and wintry Manhattan blocks to fetch my manuscript (it's a long story), and stole several of her weekend hours from her family to review and critique my work. I admire and respect your skills as a writing coach. With your encouragement I stretched as a writer and this book is the better for it.

Naomi Pauls and Gabi Proctor—the best team of copy editor and designer an author could have. My appreciation to you for your creativity, discipline and dedication to making this book the best it could be.

Robin Pascoe and Gwendolyn Gawlick who supported me from the very beginning of this process. I am so fortunate to have had my learning curve accelerated and my path made smoother because of your generosity.

All the men and women who advocated, tested and read this book in its various stages, among them Marty Avery, Jane Allison, Mitch Axelrod, Sheila Bouman, Linda Bartz, Lori Ferg, Jacqueline Foley, Sue Morris, Marilyn Ross, Monica Schweidler, Jan Stewart, Chad Theissen and Margot White. Your contribution of time and insight gave me the direction and support I needed.

The talented Briefcase Moms team—Michelle Jamison, who has been involved from the beginning, Laura Sandham and Carol Ford. Thank you for doing great work, keeping me organized and ensuring I maintained my sanity. You made my life easier.

My coach and champion Amy Ruppert, whose unshakable belief in me has been instrumental in making this book a reality. My heartfelt appreciation for your encouragement and for guiding me through the fear that originally stalled this book's movement from my mind. I can't thank you enough for holding my vision (and reminding me to) on the days I felt I no longer could.

The coaching community and all the coaches who have directly and indirectly touched my life. The "father" of coaching, the late Thomas Leonard, the faculty and leaders of Coach U and the International Coaching Federation, for giving me the tools and inspiration to do my life's work.

All my dear friends and extended family. It is difficult to thank you all individually, but know your support does not go unnoticed. Thank you for listening (and I know I talk a lot), caring for me, and traveling with me during this wild ride. Know that I am forever grateful.

My core Moms' Group—Fiona Geoghegan, Michelle Matthews, Kathy Owens and Karen Saunders—for holding me together in those first months of transition from working woman to mother to working mother. You are lifelong friends. May our children grow old together.

To my soul sister Katrina Stobbart, who walked the tightrope of working motherhood four years before me, with her daughter Tynan, and lovingly shared all her knowledge when we walked it together—she with Sage and me with Adam. Thank you for the walks, the e-mails, the dinners, the talks, the tears, the laughs, the backyard, the Boursin and the red wine.

My younger sister Nadine, the ultimate working mother, who has shown me the strength, courage and character it takes to raise three children on your own. I've learned so much from you on how to do it right. Thanks for all your advice (saving me many a trip to the emergency room at 3:00 a.m.), love and laughter.

Val and Bob Gale, my in-laws, for spoiling us with your love and time and taking such loving care of Adam from the moment he was born. Thank you for "Nana and Grandad Days."

My father, Vic Martin, who taught me that I could be anything I wanted to and has proudly supported my every endeavor.

Thomas Hawkins, my stepfather, whose talent for painting is only surpassed by the love and care he gives my mother. Thank you for being there for all of us.

The woman who is my most ardent supporter, honest advisor and compassionate sounding board, and has always reminded me of what is really important in life, my mother, Judy Hawkins. You have been my first and best working mother role model. I appreciate every minute (and there were many) you spent discussing and reviewing my manuscript and all your valuable suggestions. Thanks for showing me how important it is to share our gifts with others, for loving Robert, Adam and me unconditionally and, of course, for wearing the same shoe size.

My son, Adam. Your passion for everything continually opens my eyes to the wonder of the world. I feel so blessed that you came into my life. I love you to infinity and beyond.

My husband, Robert, my soul mate, confidante, lover and best friend, who has never allowed me to let go of my dream to write a book even though it has had a tremendous impact on his and our family life. Thank you for holding my hand and my heart through this process. Thank you for being a great father and wonderful role model for Adam. You are the best thing that has ever happened in my life.

Recommended Resources

Visit Lisa's website

The Briefcase Moms® website, www.briefcasemoms.com, is a valuable resource designed to support the busy working mother. It is jam-packed with information, assessments and tools to help you define, establish and maintain life balance.

To ensure the recommended resources for this book are as current as possible, they are being made available on the website, where they will be updated regularly.

The website also provides more information about:

- Lisa's programs and presentations
- private coaching sessions
- booking Lisa as a speaker
- purchasing a copy of this book
- quantity discounts on bulk purchases of this book,
- creating custom books, booklets, or book excerpts for specific needs, or
- how to contribute to Lisa's next book

Receive the Briefcase Moms® newsletter

When you become a member of the Briefcase Moms® revolution, you automatically get Lisa's ongoing advice and inspiration in her monthly on-line newsletter, *Briefcase Moms.*® Designed specifically to help career-oriented mothers live balanced and successful lives, it features practical lifestyle tools, articles, tips, quotes and resources to improve your work-life balance.

Share your story

Lisa welcomes the chance to learn about your journey to balance as a result of reading *Briefcase Moms.* Tell her how you are a participating in the Briefcase Moms revolution by sending her your story so she may share it with other women seeking a better balance. Seeing your success is extremely motivating for other women facing the challenges of working motherhood.

Contact Lisa at:

Lisa Martin
Founder and President
Briefcase Moms®
P.O. Box 30075, North Vancouver, B.C. Canada, V7G 1H2
Phone: 604-988-9394; Fax: 604-980-8417
Email: lisa@briefcasemoms.com

More praise for *Briefcase Moms*

"The concepts in Lisa Martin's Briefcase Moms program really helped me move forward and clarify my ideas, see my priorities and how I choose to make them fit in my life. Integrating my day job, family, the new business I am creating and me time is not easy but I now have the tools to figure out what I really want in my life. I feel much happier and more centered now."

—Lisa Kirschner, product training specialist for Triversity Inc.

"*Briefcase Moms* is like having your own personal coach in a book—a coach who helps you take a closer look at what's important and then guides you to make some positive changes to achieve a better balance."

—Jacqueline Foley, author,
Flex Appeal: An Inspirational Guide to Flexible Work for Mothers

"Lisa's Briefcase Moms program has touched my life in so many positive ways. When I felt torn between being a mom and being a business owner, Lisa helped me develop strategies to bring balance into my life. I have become a better business woman and mom!"

—Mae-Ling Tien, Founder and Mommy, Keiki Events